ENDORSEMENTS

"Anyone who claims to be self-made could have been much more if he let someone help him. The Bronner twins have created a tool to help others become better. Double Vals: The Keys to Success in College and Life Beyond is a masterful roadmap to academic excellence and holistic success. They have written a humorous and creative book that will hold the reader's attention. Double Vals is a must-read for every student as well as every person seeking a greater level of life excellence!»

-Dr. John C. Maxwell,
Speaker & New York Times Best-selling Author

"Kirstie and Kristie Bronner understand that everything we do, when we do it for God, is worthy of our greatest effort. Be inspired and challenged by Double Vals and get busy reaching your full potential in Christ."

-Steven Furtick,
Lead Pastor, Elevation Church & Author of the
New York Times bestseller Greater

"Excellence is never accidental—it is always intentional. In Double Vals: The Keys to Success in College and Life Beyond, twin sisters

Kirstie and Kristie Bronner will take you on a journey on what it takes to be double valedictorians at the prestigious Spelman College. I know them to be well rounded, non-bookish and fun-filled young ladies. Parents and young adults will find it fun reading while encouraging."

-Dr. Samuel R. Chand,
Leadership Consultant (www.samchand.com)

"The Bronner twins demonstrate that it is not what happens to you that's important. It's the way you respond to what happens to you, that's important.

These lovely young ladies would grace any intellectual and polite company. Unlike many intellectual achievers, they are not unbalanced geeks or socially impaired nerds. People of any rank of intellectuality or echelon of culture will profit enormously by reading (yes, and rereading) this book."

-Dr. John Edmund Haggai,
Founder & CEO of the Haggai Institute

"God gave Kirstie and Kristie a vision to write this book and it is written in a way that is brilliant, compelling, exciting, funny and transparent. Young people, and adults alike, will benefit from reading

this book because it serves as a reminder of the importance of being organized, setting priorities, living a balanced life, keeping a positive mind-set, and having a heart filled with faith."

-Juanchella Grooms Francis,
PhD; Spelman College Lecturer & Psychologist

"This inspirational book, Double Vals, is a great resource for students striving to pursue academic excellence and a balanced life."

-Dr. Mary J. Bailey,
Retired Executive Director/ Educational Consultant

"Double Vals is an inspirational testimony of faith and a detailed roadmap to a successful course through college and life. I wish it had been available for me to use as a resource with my students when I was a high school principal."

-Dr. Shirley C. Kilgore,
Retired Principal/Educational Leadership Consultant

"Double Vals is a remarkable, breathtaking, and heartwarming masterpiece. It will leave you with a racing heart as well as provide you with the insight to grow into the person God has always intended you to be. Kirstie and Kristie are exceptional young women of God who have woven a magnificent book to guide you through the challenges of college life. I promise you, you don't want to miss this! It is indeed a read well beyond its time!"

-Angelica Phillipps,
Sophomore at North Cobb High School, Magnet Program

"Double Vals is a not only helpful, but versatile toolbox of guidelines that will help any student, no matter what year they're in, to achieve a fulfilling and successful student career. "

-Orin Yue,
PhD Candidate at UCLA Department of Chemistry and Biochemistry

"This is an amazing book! If you have always wondered what sets the super-achievers and the rest of us apart in any area - this book holds the keys! I had only wished I had this when I was in college! This will help all students with organizational skills, time management, and more, in order to achieve holistic success in life!"

-Garrett Lee,
Singapore Management University C'2009/Staff of Heart of God Church

DOUBLE VALS

THE KEYS TO SUCCESS
IN COLLEGE AND LIFE BEYOND

KIRSTIE & KRISTIE BRONNER

Double Vals, The keys to success in college and in life beyond by Kristie and Kirstie Bronner

Published by Carnegie Books

First Edition

212 Riverside Pkwy

Austell, GA 30168

ISBN 978-0-9891356-8-9

Library of Congress Control Number: 2014903461

Front cover photography by Kyle Scott

(Canyon View Media)

CONTENTS

ACKNOWLEDGEMENTS

We want to first acknowledge God, our strength, joy, light, best friend, and main motivator. Without Jesus, we would have never had the self-discipline, dedication, and inspiration to achieve and maintain 4.0 GPA's. Without that accomplishment, this book would not exist!

It's amazing how God does everything for a reason, and when you surrender your life to Christ completely, He will take you to places you could have never imagined.

To our parents: We literally could not have completed this book without you two! You both have encouraged us so much and have helped to push us to get this done in the midst of everything else on our plates. Without your support, reminders, prayers, and help along the way, this book would not be available right now.

Mom, you are the best mother that anyone could ever ask for! You love not only in word and tongue, but in deed and in truth (1 John 3:18). Your encouragement helps us to keep going even when we feel discouraged. You assist us in so many ways, and you do it with joy and kindness that is amazing! You are a helpful angel to us, our role model, our friend, and oh yeah, the best mom in the world!

Dad, your example of excellence is astounding! Your wisdom has shaped our mindsets. So much of who you are is found in us and in this book! Your support has provided opportunities for us that we may have never otherwise experienced. You truly are the best father that anyone could ask for! Thank you for your love, your encouragement, and for just being who you are. You prophesied our destinies before we ever saw it and called our gifts into manifestation!

Parents like you two are rare and precious beyond words. Your support, resources, time, encouragement, and love don't go unnoticed one bit. You will never rot in a nursing home with no teeth, urine odors, or abuse! Ha ha! We love ya'll!

To Dr. Francis: You are God-sent to our lives! Our mentor, our counselor, and our 2nd mom—you are truly amazing! You continue to bless us like you'll never know, and your help and sacrifices have demonstrated your love beyond words. We are so appreciative for all that you are to us! Your support, affirmation, wisdom, guidance, humor, and example add so much to our lives. We pray that God will bless you, your family, and your ministry beyond your wildest dreams!

To our Word of Faith Family: Thank you so much for your love, support, and prayers throughout our lives that have helped us to achieve what we have thus far. You all are amazing!

To Dr. Cornejo: Thank you for your great help in this process as our kind, excellent art designer. God bless you and all of your future endeavors!

LIGHTS, CAMERA, ACTION!:

FROM THE CLASSROOM TO THE HEADLINES

Flashing lights in a sea of cameras, questions hollered by eager reporters, and towering skyscrapers in the Big Apple are what we faced as we exited the glistening black Escalade. "O-M-G, I hope I don't look too crazy adjusting my dress as I stand up…and I definitely hope they don't catch on camera this run up my thigh before I can get my dress pulled all the way down on my way out this car!... Man, this is so cool! I didn't know the paparazzi would be out here waiting for us like this. I feel like a celebrity, and I'm just *me*!"—Thoughts racing through our minds as we stepped out of the vehicle in front of the *Fox and Friends* studio.

Everything was happening so fast! One minute we are in Atlanta, Georgia, and the next moment we are in New York City sitting in the waiting room with one of the Disney Channel stars, Ashley Tisdale, from *The Suite Life of Zack and Cody*. Yes, we couldn't help ourselves: We got our camera phones out and took a picture with her before we went on the show. We were excited and nervous as we headed onstage.

Sitting under the bright lights of the impressive television studio, gazing at the huge TV equipment and the celebrity host, we can't help but feel overwhelmingly blessed! What a whirlwind of exciting, yet nerve-racking opportunities for us! Hoping to make family and friends who are watching proud; praying that we will present ourselves in a way that we personally will be pleased to look back on; excited about the amazing opportunity; hoping that every hair is still in place and that our lip gloss is still poppin' for the camera: it's time to go on live! Oh, the thoughts and pictures in our minds during this first experience of its kind!

OPPORTUNITIES GALORE

Lights, camera, ACTION!!! The opportunities just kept on coming. Within two weeks of our graduation, we were called for approximately 20 different interviews! Most of these were requests for next day interviews, and often we were doing two to three interviews a day. We were all over the Internet, news channels, radio, magazines, newspapers, blogs, YouTube, and social networks. Imagine our shock when we went to check our email and saw ourselves featured on Yahoo News! Someone even showed us the ridiculous comments about us on *WorldStarHipHop*!

It was as if we became national celebrities overnight! Instead of church members around the city saying, "You're Bishop Bronner's daughters, aren't you?!," there were people of all cultures exclaiming, "You're the valedictorian twins from TV!" It was surprising to us just how interested everyone was in our story.

KEYS FROM OUR STORY

What is success if you can't share it with others? We've realized that God has given us keys to successful habits because He wants us to share them with the world. This book is our way to share in detail much of the wisdom and strategy that God graced us with in order to maintain perfect GPA's, while finding balance and life fulfillment.

In Appendix A you will find a list of media sources from many different states, and even countries, that displayed our story. We were SHOCKED when we saw this list ourselves about five months later! We didn't even know about most of these headlines! Our desire is that after studying this book, you will be equipped to achieve your ultimate success academically and in every other area of life. You never know where doing your best will take you (We sure didn't!)...

CHAPTER 1

OUR STORY:

A LOOK INTO OUR TWIN WORLD, FAMILY, & MOTIVATION

Since we can remember, the two of us have lived very different lives from the average person, partially because we are twins and partially because we are pastor's kids, a.k.a., PK's. We've always received a lot of attention, whether flattering or annoying. At the most basic level, we are always asked the famous question, "Hey, are you girls twins?" Hmm… We are identical, we are dressed alike, and our hair is exactly the same… What could have given it away??? (scratching our heads) Just a thought…

To add to the attention, our father is the senior pastor and founder of an over 20,000-member church, called Word of Faith Family Worship Cathedral in Austell, GA. Although it has not always been this large, it has always been a good-sized, healthy, home-like, and growing church.

For some reason, people think pastor's kids are either supposed

to be Jesus or demons in disguise, but that's a whole other story...
We are neither. We're just youth trying to live life serving God
and fulfilling His purpose. (Do you know that church people have
approached us at the movies with our boyfriends, saying, "I was
watching you in there and I am so proud of you! I will tell your
parents you behaved well!" Yes, they did. Ha ha! We do love our
church members, though. They mean well and love generously.)

Whether we received attention at church or in public for being the
pastor's daughters, twins, or because of physical attraction, we have
always been showered with an abundance of attention. Of course,
the degree of attention has increased significantly with the publicity
about this whole double valedictorian thing. Our story takes a look
into our twin world, our family background, our motivation, and
how our success story can become yours.

TWIN WORLD

To give a little more background, we will give you a sneak peek inside of the world of an identical twin by sharing the most common and corny twin jokes we continue to hear regularly. It's funny how each person thinks they are the first one to make that particular joke. Many times, we've heard, "Is this a mirror? Hee hee hee!" "Didn't I just see you? Uha ha ha ha!" "Do you know what she is thinking right now? Hardy harr harr!" "How old are you…? Okay, now how old are you…? Ah ha ha!" "If you get hit, does the other twin feel it? Mwa ha ha!"

Some other things aren't common, simply strange. One time, we were walking briskly through the mall because we were in a rush, and a lady who was working at one of the mall stands stopped us and stared at us, trying to examine our features and figure out the differences between us. She then pulled one of us on one side of the mall directory and the other on the other side and asked us to switch and see if she could still tell the difference. Interestingly enough, she didn't even know our names, so how could she possibly begin to distinguish us?! Imagine being in a rush, and someone stops you to stare at your face for a long time while simultaneously treating you like a child and a zoo animal—not fun!

Often, we find ourselves in the same awkward situation, merely different folks conducting this weird display. Imagine someone in your face, yet speaking to someone else ABOUT you. "Aww, they are so cute!" "Look at them, they look just alike!" "Oh my goodness, they are just adorable, and they still dress alike!" "I wonder if their parents get them confused." "I wonder which one is older." These kinds of statements made to others in our faces remove us from the conversation while they talk ABOUT us. It is as if we are babies who can't speak yet, or as if we are fish behind glass in an aquarium. They actually could just ask us, you know. After all, we kinda are the ones with the answers to these questions, not their friends.

When discussing annoying attention, we cannot forget a situation that happened when we were about seventeen years old. We were at a friend's birthday dinner when a young lady, probably sixteen, sat in front of us with her boyfriend. For an entire thirty minutes or more, she stared at us. Once again, we experienced the feeling of being fish behind aquarium glass. She talked to her boyfriend ABOUT us, directly in front of us at the table, and the encounter went something like the following:

Girl: "Oh my gosh, they look just alike! So much that it's almost scary. I always thought twins were like aliens or something... Have you ever thought that, baby? Aww man... I think they really are from Mars!"

Boyfriend: "Yeah, I think they are definitely from Mars!"

Us: "We can hear you, ya know..."

Girl whispering to boyfriend: "Oh my goodness, baby, they said they can hear us!"

(a little while later aloud…)

Girl: "OMG! I think I can tell the difference now… One of their noses goes a little bit up like this (pressing her nose up to look like a pig), and the other one's goes a little bit down like this (smashing her nose down to look deformed)."

Imagine this encounter lasting approximately 30 minutes… Now imagine our facial expressions and thoughts this whole time… We were sensitive about every twin joke for quite some time after this!

Finally, although that instance was rare and cruel, there are very common twin experiences that all twins despise, which can be summed up in one word—comparisons. People ask questions of comparison that are clearly inappropriate to ask anyone, but especially not appropriate to ask twins, since twins typically battle with issues of comparison and competition their entire lives! Some of the questions are, "Who's the smartest?" "Who's the bossy twin?" "Who's the good twin, and who's the bad twin? There's always a good one and a bad one!"

Others observe and compare in an attempt to find our differences through intense study… For example, true story… "I got it now!!! Your face is fat and your face is skinny! Your voice is deep like a bass and yours is high! I got it! I got it!" As absurd as these statements sound, we have heard them countless times throughout our lives, particularly from people over the age of thirty who should know better. Human nature is an interesting phenomenon. Therefore, by the love of Christ, we must continually "forgive them, for they know not what they do." ☺

Don't get us wrong, though. We actually love being twins! There is certainly more good than bad. I mean, who wouldn't love to be given your best friend in the womb! Someone to make almost every life transition easier because they are in it with you… Someone who understands exactly how you feel because they often feel the same way, and someone to share your passions and interests with who complements you, helping you to be an even better you…

People wonder if we ever fight because we are so close. I have one question… Are we humans sharing the same living quarters?… question answered. Nevertheless, we don't argue long because we understand each other's true intentions. We share interests, hobbies, favorite foods, talents, and even characteristics, but we are separate people with differing personalities who just happen to be best friends for life.

ALWAYS DIFFERENT

We have never been able to blend in. At church, we were sometimes outcasts among the other children in our pre-teen and early teenage years. Interestingly, we were often ridiculed by other kids, at church, for attributes of our faith. Peers AT CHURCH negatively talked about us because we chose not to listen to secular music, attend wild parties, drink alcohol, or have pre-marital sex. Nevertheless, our faith was and forever will be a worthy cause to deal with any kind of isolation. After all, it is the most important part of life. Christ is life!

Of course, it didn't help that we were pastor's kids and homeschooled since fifth grade. To be clear, we were not taught our academics by our mom, but through an accredited program using recorded classes from an excellent school. They mailed our DVDs, quizzes, tests, and books, and we mailed back our completed work and progress reports in exchange for our official report cards. We were not forced into homeschool like young prisoners on lock-down. We actually requested to be homeschooled because we had homeschooled friends!

Also, our social life was limited in our earlier days, not because of being homeschooled, but because we were extremely shy. In late middle school and high school, though, we came out of our shells and spent just about every weekend hanging out at the mall with friends like every other teenager! We did, however, still have many habits that you will soon learn which caused us to always stand out (in positive ways).

Even when it came to college graduation, we were surprised about, once again, being pulled out from among the rest. We were happy, yet nervous, when we were told that, for the first time in numerous years, the valedictorian was going to give a speech at the graduation ceremony. It had been Spelman's tradition to have only the class president speak to represent the class at graduation. Isn't it something that we ended up making history as the double vals the same year that the administration decided to change the rules?!

When we realized that we had to sit on the stage because we were valedictorians, we were unpleasantly surprised. We didn't want that kind of spotlight throughout a three-hour ceremony in which we honestly had experienced drowsiness in previous years (As glee club members, we sang at graduation every year.). The thought of dosing off on stage in front of thousands of people was a frightening daydream! We also wanted to sit with our classmates on such a special day, but, for some reason, God has always had us set apart for reasons we have come to greatly appreciate.

INTRINSIC MOTIVATION

Contrary to what most assume, we did not excel academically because of pressure from our parents. In fact, nothing positive that we have done or established in our own lives (including such choices as only listening to Christian music) has been because our parents placed pressure upon us, making us feel as if we wouldn't be acceptable without meeting certain standards. They simply instilled the correct values in us, nurtured us, encouraged us, and praised us when we did well. They trained us up in the way we should go

(Prov. 22:6) and then allowed us to make our own decisions with their guidance.

Some believe that after achieving 4.0's in the beginning of college, we must have felt intense pressure to keep that GPA, making it our fuel to work hard. Another common thought is that we competed with each other academically. Truthfully, we both have always been internally motivated to the degree that no one else could possibly pressure us more than we pressured ourselves. This idea can be explained in the terms *self-discipline and intrinsic motivation.* We have always been taught in our home to be excellent and do our best in all that we do. Therefore, even in the classroom, we felt the need to do our best in everything and surpass average.

Every time people told us, "Don't take that teacher because she's hard and no one makes an 'A' in her class," we took the teacher anyway and proved that we can do all things through Christ who strengthens us (Philippians 4:13). We chose classes based upon which classes interested us the most and which ones we felt that we could learn the most valuable information from.

We did not allow ourselves to be deterred by another student who was not willing to go the extra mile in class. We were not satisfied with each assignment until we were confident that we had given it our all and that it was the best we could do. Simply put, we were so driven to excellence that we felt very uncomfortable and out of place when we didn't perform at our best.

GENIUS OR WORKER?

Before we entered college, we always thought that someone who had a 4.0 GPA was a genius! Who would've ever thought that we would both graduate with 4.0's without cheating and without being double geniuses? We actually were very insecure about our academic ability when entering college. We believe that insecurity was one of the motivators of our hard work initially. We felt that we needed to do more in an effort to, not only measure up, but to excel.

In our adolescent years, we told our mother that we didn't think we were smart enough to attend her Alma Mater, Spelman College. We felt this way because it was a private school, and because we had heard that the admission process was very selective and the curriculum was very challenging. As expected, she told us that we were very intelligent and could attend any school of our choice.

• • •

THE HIGHEST REWARDS ARE NOT ALWAYS ATTRIBUTED TO THE SMARTEST OR TO THE MOST CONFIDENT; BUT THOSE WHO PRAY, STRATEGIZE, AND WORK HARD OFTEN RISE TO THE TOP

• • •

Since we were homeschooled, we questioned our academic competence in comparison to other students in the traditional classroom. Our mother always told us that we were very capable of competing with other students, but we continued to doubt. Home school did, however, cause us to practice self-discipline and time management, as was necessary, to stay abreast of all our work without the hounding of a teacher. This discipline has worked to our advantage as we have learned first-hand that the highest rewards are not always attributed to the smartest or to the most confident; but those who pray, strategize, and work hard often rise to the top.

USEFUL LIFE STRATEGIES

The reason our academic success can be taught is that it came not from natural genius but from those three concepts—prayer, strategy, and hard work. Anyone is capable of applying the principles we will share in this book and experiencing drastic results in school, at work, and in life success. Learning such skills as scheduling, balance, and perspective never become un-useful.

It is interesting to note that the same keys to success in school can follow you and aid you throughout life. After college, we realized that what we learned in college about balancing schoolwork, time, and life in order to produce excellence, health, and joy, are the same principles that we need in everyday life. For example, the evening glee club rehearsals, after a long day of classes and schoolwork, prepared us for the evening rehearsals and programs that we now conduct during the week after already working in the daytime. All of it was preparation!

During our college years, we used to wonder why we couldn't have more free time in our schedule, but now we are grateful for the discipline and balance we learned. At least now what we spend our time doing is our purpose and passion, and therefore, our pleasure to pencil in!

For those who did not learn the keys to success in school, it's not too late! You will often find procrastinators from school days still procrastinating on work-related tasks. You can also discover the same people who "half-did" everything academically, "half-doing" things professionally. Truth is truth! Whatever personality traits or lack of strategy you might have felt were hindering your success can all be in the past!

You, with God's help, have the power to change whatever it is that you don't like about yourself or your habits and move towards your highest level of productivity, effectiveness, and ultimately, well-balanced success! Whatever you refuse to accept, you can adjust. Keep reading to learn strategies for improvement in many worthwhile areas!

• • •
WHATEVER YOU REFUSE TO ACCEPT, YOU CAN ADJUST
• • •

CHAPTER 2

THE ART OF BALANCED LIVING

KEY: PRODUCTIVITY+PLAY+PRAYER = HEALTH

O ur first Christmas break during college was magnificent! We went to the mall almost every day, watched lots of movies, made many tacos (our favorite food), and were completely immersed in relaxation! We didn't have a care in the world. The only problem we faced was the harsh reality of our marvelous break coming to a close…

When our first Christmas break was quickly fleeting, we realized that we had to do something different. Dread filled our hearts as we anticipated the next semester because of the stress that accompanied the very memory of school… What was the missing ingredient in the midst of our perfect GPA's first semester? Balance!

OUR JOURNEY

Both of us began Spelman College without balance. We prioritized our schoolwork, and we fulfilled our responsibilities to the great, yet time-consuming Spelman College Glee Club. Unfortunately, we were studyaholics. In our first semester of college, we studied every hour we were not in class, including nights and entire weekends. We became burned out. We were unhappy during the semester, always saying, "I can't wait until Christmas break!" After that vacation period, our daily beam of hope became, "Summer break is-a-comin'!"

We were waiting until a certain point to begin enjoying life, instead of learning to enjoy every day and to enjoy the journey. Not only were we unhappy during this time period, but we were also unhealthy. The extreme stress we endured impaired our immune systems and caused us to retain colds for our entire first semester. Both of us caught a new cold before the symptoms of the previous one could disappear.

• • •

As YOU ARE ENJOYING THE JOURNEY OF LIFE, YOU SHOULD WORK HARD BUT ALWAYS SET SOMETHING TO LOOK FORWARD TO

• • •

The glee club had a seating corner for those with colds so that they could learn the music without infecting others. It was called "the sick corner." We were sick the whole semester! After the first couple of times in the sick corner, we just said to ourselves, "Shoot, we can't sit there all semester, so we might as well go back to our seats now!" We coughed the entire semester. Upon entrance to the second semester, we realized that something's gotta give: this way of living was just too stressful to repeat.

By the second semester, we still battled stress, but each semester became better than the one before. We purposefully pursued balance and health along with a perfect grade point average. Because our natural tendency was to overwork ourselves, we began to schedule our relaxation and our fun with friends during certain hours of the weekends. In fact, as you are enjoying the journey of life, you should work hard but always set something to look forward to. Having this in mind provides more energy for the present. Therefore, we made sure we did something fun every weekend, regardless of how much work we had. Scheduled recreation became priority!

For example, one Saturday we had planned to attend a fun event with our church youth group from 3 p.m. to 10 p.m. As the event drew nearer, we realized that we needed to be working on a paper that Saturday. Therefore, we set our alarm for 5 a.m. Saturday (although it seemed outrageous), and we headed to the library. When it was time to go to the event, we had already spent the number of hours that we would have normally spent in a day on that paper. Yes, we planned ahead and worked to get both the paper and the recreation activity into our day.

Of course, we know that most people's struggle is not too little relaxation, but too darn much! This is due to insufficient self-discipline, probably accompanying a Type B personality, discussed later in this chapter. **Regardless of your primary inclination, be determined to implement the necessary balance for a healthy and productive life.**

PERSONALITY TENDENCIES

Friend: "Girl, you do not need to be doin' no work on Friday night!" (our laid-back friend's attempt to advise us to relax freshman year)

"I probably need to do some work tomorrow, though, since I couldn't break away from the TV this week."

Us (on Monday): "Did you get your work done this weekend?"

Friend: "Nah girl, I ended up hanging with my boo this weekend. I guess I'll skip class and rehearsal today to finish it tonight, hee hee hee. It sho' was fun tho'! What about ya'll? Did ya'll take Friday off?"

Us: "Well… after we wrote the rough draft of our ADW paper…"

Different personality types have varying natural tendencies toward certain behaviors that lead to either side of the spectrum. Those with Type A personalities tend to be more aggressive, competitive, ambitious, and stressed. The same qualities that drive them to meet deadlines early, to always arrive to obligations in a timely fashion, and to be distinct in their natural leadership ability, also tend to generate more nervousness, anxiety, stress, and general workaholic symptoms.

Those who exhibit Type B personalities are more relaxed and easy-going. The same qualities that keep them stress-free and comfortable in pressure-generating situations sometimes cause them to be too passive for maximum productivity.

If you have not yet become intentional in your efforts to be balanced, you must first recognize whether you are more prone to being stressed or prone to being passive. Then, you strategize in your area of lack.

We acknowledged our tendency to overwork and stress, so we intentionally scheduled time for relaxation. Those who tend to relax too often and give too little time to their studies must purposefully schedule their academics so that their schedules become more strict and organized.

Regardless of your personality, each of us has tendencies that create the need for us to purposefully adjust our behavior to maintain a healthy balance. Identify your tendencies and strategize.

• • •
*I*DENTIFY YOUR
TENDENCIES AND
STRATEGIZE
• • •

LESSONS FROM ITALY

"Hakuna matata!" For those who have seen the classic Disney film, *Lion King*, you know that this term means "no worries for the rest of your days!" As Timon and Pumbaa stated, "It's a problem-free philosophy!"

Our semester in Italy taught us a valuable lesson of life balance that we will never forget. We found ourselves reciting the term, *Hakuna matata*, several times because of what it represented. It was our regular reminder of the lesson that the Italian culture taught us to incorporate in our own American culture.

To be honest, both the Italian and the American cultures are generally off-balance. Some of the Italians told us this saying: "Italians work to live; but, Americans live to work." In essence, some Italians think of Americans as being obsessed with their work. Although the stereotypes of each culture are not 100% true for everyone, they definitely hold truth.

Italians have a beautiful emphasis on family and friends. For them, mealtime is a prime opportunity to catch up on each other's daily lives, invest in relationships, and EAT in the midst of love and laughter. It is not uncommon to find Italians taking 1 ½-2-hour lunch breaks. Some of our Italian friends there said this: "If you see someone walking and eating at the same time, they are not Italian!"

Americans, on the other hand, eat while walking all the time! Why? Because we tend to be the kings and queens of convenience. Americans typically take 30-minute to 1-hour lunch breaks so that they can more quickly return to work. It is also very uncommon to find American families hosting large dinners during the week "just because." For Americans, it is usually a special occasion if we schedule something like that to happen…maybe a birthday or Thanksgiving.

Some of our time in Italy, we found ourselves struggling with incorporating the Italian customs. For example, when our Italian roommates would plan a dinner for the apartment, we sometimes battled our emotions about losing the time we would have spent doing schoolwork, sleeping, or Skyping friends and family back home.

Our daily schedules included leaving school to go to the grocery store (Italians typically grocery shop every day or every other day because their food perishes quickly.), going to our separate apartments, doing our homework while eating dinner, Skyping people from home, and then sleeping. A 3-hour apartment dinner was sometimes difficult for us to wrap our minds around.

Despite our self-imposed friction, we made adjustments to cooperate when asked by our Italian roommates. To one another, we discussed the differences in typical American culture versus that of Italy. We made it our point to put into practice "Hakuna matata," which somewhat described the Italian way of thinking. After returning to America, we comically repeated this term every time it seemed that stress began to knock on our door. Try this with a close friend or roommate only if your tendency is to over-work and stress. ☺

The best way to have a good balance is to take note of the valuable elements of each culture. From Americans, adopt ambition and strong organizational skills. From Italians, adopt the value of family, friends, and stress-free living. One good way to balance the mealtime idea is to schedule at least one day out of the week to have a nice, planned meal with family/friends. For example, we faithfully attend our large family dinner on Sundays. If you don't live near family, do the same with meaningful friendships. You will be surprised by the difference it will make in your weeks!

YOU WANT IT? SCHEDULE IT.

In order to purposefully achieve balance, we must schedule it. This means scheduling the hours you will spend on work for school or for your career, as well as scheduling the hours you will spend having fun, relaxing, and sleeping. **When you schedule the time, unless there are emergencies, you cannot say that you did not have the time.**

We purposefully schedule all work and engagements around church, family dinners, and even some recreational activities with friends. That way, we can make sure that it happens! For those who spend too much time on fun activities, in order to achieve greater academic success, they must schedule far more time for academics than they

• • •
*I*N ORDER TO PURPOSEFULLY ACHIEVE BALANCE, WE MUST SCHEDULE IT
• • •

do currently. All other activities should only occur outside of this allotted time.

With proper scheduling of other priorities, you can even achieve a consistently sufficient sleep schedule. Sufficient sleep will keep you alert, energized, and ready to perform to the best of your ability in your academic endeavors and extra curricular activities.

When you do not schedule properly, you end up "pulling all-nighters" to accomplish goals at the last minute. This can cause additional stress because, when you lose sleep to finish assignments at the last minute, you risk not finishing on time, submitting mediocre or sloppy work, formulating questions that you have no time to get answered by the instructor, and developing unhealthy habits.

Some students report that they work better under pressure; however, this kind of personal experience does not eliminate the risks involved, nor does it guarantee quality work or sufficient rest. You must schedule properly so that you can balance the time in your days in the most effective way.

NEED FOR BALANCE: CASE STUDY

There are some people in this world who can be classified as extremists. Every new hobby they begin and every emotion they express is exaggerated. They are what many would consider to be "overboard." They are either on one side or the other and give all of their energy to one thing at a time, leaving no time or thought for other important elements of life. Moderation is a foreign concept to this kind of person.

A more recognizable example of an extremist looks like the person who begins a new business endeavor, and there is all of a sudden no more time for family, eating balanced meals, or even sleeping. Another extremist takes YOLO (You only live once.) to the ultimate extent! He/she lives a wild, unplanned, and unwise existence, while damaging relationships, health, and finances. All this chaos is in the name of fun, feeling, adventure, and relaxation—aloha bruhder (as if you're always on vacation)! This extremist idea that we speak of is not as uncommon as you may think. It merely exists at varying levels. These examples represent the absence of a healthy and balanced life.

Let's take a look at two guys that demonstrate this concept. Brandon and Jake represent clear opposites of the personality spectrum. Brandon was a quiet Type A personality. He was what some people would call a hermit and workaholic. He had no close friendships, and he didn't invest significant time in his family relationships. Between his jobs at McDonald's and H&M, his weekends were packed. He didn't attend any Sunday church service, no Friday night movie with friends, and no scheduled family dinners. He did, however, attend every class and work obligation. Brandon made straight A's in school and has been employee of the month on both of his jobs at least twice in the past 6 months.

Jake, on the other hand, was Mr. Social Butterfly. He was an outgoing Type B personality. Ever since college orientation, he was a people magnet. Jake was never afraid to try new things. He grew up fairly sheltered, so when he got to college, he "made the most of it" in his own mind. He tried wild parties, drinking contests, marijuana, and sexual promiscuity. Nothing was off-limits for him to try, except for self-discipline. Jake rarely attended his classes, failed to turn in several assignments, and had no job. His grades significantly reflected his poor work ethic.

Brandon ended up with ulcers in his body because of the constant stress. Without regular release of the stress, his body responded in a way that was damaging to his health. On the other hand, Jake ended up with three STD's, an addiction to marijuana, and a loss of his academic scholarship. Neither Brandon nor Jake was content.

Balance is necessary for ultimate success in life because life is a journey, not a destination. Our initial problem was no academic balance. We worked. We worked. Then, when we finished working, we worked some more. We burned out. Therefore, as you strive for your

• • •

IT IS IMPORTANT TO HAVE THE KIND OF BALANCE THAT MAKES LIFE PRODUCTIVE AND ENJOYABLE AT THE SAME TIME

• • •

goals and overall mission, you must make sure to maintain balance in all areas of life for overall health and success.

It is important to have the kind of balance that makes life productive and enjoyable at the same time. Without proper balance, people end up with 4.0 GPA's and abundant material possessions but failing physical health and damaged relationships. Others' imbalance may result in strong relationships and good health but low GPA's and poor financial conditions.

SPIRITUAL REJUVENATION

As important as work, sleep, relaxation, and fun are to balanced living, you must have balance in your spiritual life as well. You cannot fully be balanced in your life if you do not make time for spiritual development. Having a daily scheduled time for devotion with God (prayer and Bible reading), in addition to weekly church attendance, not only helps you to build and maintain your relationship with God, but it also serves as a mental and emotional release in the midst of stressful experiences.

If you do not schedule your spiritual rejuvenation, it is easy to get distracted and seem to run out of time. One simple way to ensure that you don't neglect to prioritize your spiritual life is by doing your devotional time in the morning before school or work. If you do this before you even leave the house or take care of other obligations, there is no such thing as not having time for it.

To be a well-rounded individual, you must purposefully feed yourself spiritually on a regular basis.

CHALLENGE

1. Identify your tendencies to be off-balance.

- Do you tend to be so relaxed and worry-free that you don't have sufficient motivation to work diligently and efficiently?

- Are you so driven that you don't regularly give yourself adequate time to unwind?

- Do you neglect your mental, physical, emotional, or spiritual health?

- Do you neglect your important relationships?

- Do you make time for spiritual investment?

2. Establish what you will do differently for the coming week to achieve balance in the necessary areas.

CHAPTER 3

HOW TO OUT-SMART TIME:

The Keys to Time Management

KEY: PAY NOW; PLAY LATER.

"Well, what had happened was… I was planning to study today, but Eric and Stephanie invited me to the movies… The next day, I planned to pick up the slack, but then Scandal came on, and you know I couldn't resist my show! I ended up with so many things that I had pushed to the back-burner in my mind, that I actually forgot about some of my assignments. I got sleepy last night, so I had to just go to bed, and in the morning between my classes, I got in the best, but long, conversation! Dog gonnet! I am always running out of time…"

Time management seems to be one of the most significant challenges that college students encounter when approaching schoolwork. In fact, this same struggle often continues beyond college when it is not conquered in this environment. While attempting to manage academic work, participate in extracurricular activities, engage in social and recreational activities, sleep, and eat, college students commonly fail to plan appropriately. As a result, sleep deprivation, unhealthy eating habits, procrastination with academics, and stress often accompany the life of the average student.

SELF-DISCIPLINE

Pay now; play later. This key is rooted in self-discipline. We know that it doesn't sound very fun, but you've got to trust, it is worth it! Discipline is a gift that some people possess. For others, this skill must be developed.

We must admit that even though we are humans who get tired and restless sometimes, God certainly graced us with self-discipline. We did not feel comfortable enjoying certain pleasures if we had not finished what we planned to accomplish. For example, during one semester, there was a TV show we loved so much that it was the only one we made time for once a week! We were so disciplined that, even though the show came on at 10 p.m., we did not feel comfortable just taking the time to watch it.

This semester was an extremely heavy workload, so in order to uphold our academic standards and weekend priorities, we often worked until 11 or 12 p.m. nightly after glee club rehearsal. Therefore, in an effort to stay on our schedule, we waited until 10 p.m. to eat dinner the one night a week our show came on, just so that we could eat and watch our show simultaneously, killing two birds with one stone!

Of course, we ate snacks while we worked so that we wouldn't completely starve, but we sacrificed to manage our time most effectively. As a result of making the necessary sacrifices during the week, we were able to get 6-7 hours of sleep most nights, achieve our academic goals, and maintain our priorities of church, family dinner, and some recreation with friends on the weekends.

Self-discipline can simply be thought of as the practice of doing what you need to do until you can do what you want to do. In reality, you can do whatever you want to do at any point. The consequences of obeying personal desire in inappropriate timing include disorganization, laziness, lack of productivity, frustration, and stress. Simply put, doing what you feel like doing instead of what you should be doing leads to these undesirable outcomes.

To have the most effective self-discipline, you must sharpen it with wise strategies, regular practice, and consistent prayer. **One strategy that helps with self-discipline is to set short-term goals and incentives along the way to the long-term**

• • •

*S*ELF-DISCIPLINE CAN SIMPLY BE THOUGHT OF AS THE PRACTICE OF DOING WHAT YOU NEED TO DO UNTIL YOU CAN DO WHAT YOU WANT TO DO

• • •

goals. This strategy works even when dealing with goals such as finishing a long reading assignment for school.

For example, as an incentive, you could tell yourself that after every ten pages, you will eat a snack, send a text message, check your social media, call a friend on the phone, take a nap, or do whatever relaxes and refreshes you temporarily. Remember, whatever you choose must be held to a strict time limit!

When using strategies such as these, you must be careful to continue with only the incentives that work for you. If you find that checking social media for five minutes quickly becomes an hour, try something else. **Avoid addictive break activities such as television, video games, or going out with friends during the week**.

What has just been explained is another point in time management— scheduling breaks. Scheduling breaks throughout the day is essential to self-discipline because **if you do not schedule the break, you will most likely end up taking a break anyway**. These **unplanned breaks tend to be long and addictive**. Your brain needs breaks built into heavy study time and tedious assignments, but you must be intentional about them (See "Study Breaks" in the "Nerdy Nuggets for 100%" chapter for more details.)

Learn how to say "no" to most activities that interrupt your schedule. If friends ask about going to lunch somewhere off-campus that you know will turn into a hangout in the middle of the day, just politely say, "No thanks. I need to stay here and…" The same applies to when people ask about going to hang out in the evenings during the week. **Remain focused on your priorities during the week, and then take time to socialize and relax during the weekends**.

This is when you must remain confident in your identity. Regardless of what people assume about you, remind yourself of the purpose for being in school. Yes, people will start calling you a nerd and saying you never go out anywhere, blah blah blah… Nevertheless, people will admire the excellence of your results, and your real friends will learn to understand and respect your intentions. They will hang out with you during the weekends.

Concerning meal invitations, you can and should have meals on campus with your friends during the week. We all need to be social. Nevertheless, your new time management skills will cause you to always **give yourself a time limit and stick to it**. ☺

Note: Sometimes, you will have an offer about something besides academics that deserves sacrifice. For instance, if you have a friend who is in a crisis and hurting, you should stop, pray, and offer counsel. If you are a musician and someone offers you a significant gig during the week, you should not make a habit of declining opportunities that could propel you.

Just make sure that, on these occasions, you do what is necessary to complete your schoolwork, whether you must stay up later, work more on the weekend, or decline one of your usual activities. **You must learn to pray and weigh**. Pause to ask God to lead you to the right decision and then weigh the pros and cons.

TO-DO LIST TO THE RESCUE!

Do you ever have the feeling that your mind is racing, that so many things are coming to mind that you can barely focus on what you are currently doing? Sometimes this invasion of thoughts will occur while you are reading, showering, driving, getting dressed, or even in class. You suddenly think of every errand you need to run, every person you need to ask a clarifying question, every assignment that is coming up soon, and even the laundry that you need to wash. You can't possibly handle all of these tasks at the moment you are in class or in the bathroom, so what do you do? Write them down.

> • • •
> *THE MORE THAT YOU RECORD ON PAPER, THE LESS THAT HAS TO REMAIN ON YOUR MIND AT A GIVEN TIME*
> • • •

Whenever you start to feel a lot of things come to your mind that you have to do, start writing. **The more that you record on paper, the less that has to remain on your mind at a given time**. When you fail to write down the many different errands, assignments, and other tasks that flood your mind, you will forget some of them. If you hold tightly to them in your mind, you will move more slowly and less effectively with whatever you are currently doing. These ideas and imminent tasks that you jot down become your to-do list.

Making a to-do list is imperative to an organized, productive day. Without a to-do list, knowing when to say "no" to time-wasting activities is not as clear. **A list helps you remain mindful of the goals for the day so that forgetfulness is not the cause of failing to meet daily goals.** Therefore, you should first decide which items of your list must be completed today and which ones can be done another day. Then create a timeline for your goals for the day. This order helps to eliminate wasting time because you plan ahead the time restrictions for each goal in order to wisely organize your day.

Small sticky notes are ideal because, after you have crossed out the completed goals for that day and/or week, you can easily remove them and throw the old lists away. These lists should be very detailed, including the time allotted for particular assignments, errands, and routine activities such as meals, travel time, prayer, and Bible reading.

In order to be most organized, productive, and balanced, you must decide what your priorities are and make the necessary sacrifices to accommodate these priorities. For example, if spending time with family is your priority, put them on your to-do list, and pencil them in! When we were in college, our family lived 45 minutes away from us, but, as we said, every Sunday (unless we had a glee club performance), we went to dinner with them. Your family might not be local, but you can schedule a weekly phone conversation. In addition, developing a certain skill might be a priority for you. Put it on the list, and give it an appointment and a time limit.

Certain assignments take priority over others because of due date and the percentage of your grade that applies to it. **Make your to-do list holistic, but realistic and in order of importance**. For instance, after you have scribbled everything that is on your mind onto your sticky note, rewrite the list in order of importance. Because maximum productivity and success in academics are your priorities, and because efficiency of time usage (a.k.a. time management) is required for best results, you must use your minutes wisely.

STUDY OR SLEEP TIME?

6:00 a.m., BUZZZZ, Snooze…
6:15 a.m., BUZZZZ, Snooze…
6:30 a.m., BUZZZZ, Snooze…
7:00 a.m., BUZZZZ, Snooze…
7:30 a.m., BUZZZZ, Snooze…
9:00 a.m., BUZZZZ, Snooze…
And so on…

This cycle of sleeping later than planned or later than what *should* have been planned, might be okay for some Saturdays, but not for the weekday mornings. Imagine what you could have accomplished in that additional 30 minutes, 1 hour, 2 hours that you snoozed…

Sleeping late is one element that students should sacrifice in order to squeeze more productivity from each day. Remember that **the things you do differently make you different**. It might seem tough, but **if you want to excel above the rest, develop exceptional habits**. This is how an average mind produces genius results! Here is a general tip—if your first class of the day begins later than 10 a.m., wake up early enough to get some things done before class— that is, if your mind is most clear, focused, and refreshed in the morning.

During our sophomore year at Spelman, we had a class that began at 10 a.m. This was the first time that we had a class this late because, up to this point, we were accustomed to classes that began at 8 a.m. or 9 a.m. This particular semester of our first 10 a.m. class, we were concerned that we might lose efficiency in our time management if we started our day later.

> • • •
> *If* YOU WANT TO EXCEL ABOVE THE REST, DEVELOP EXCEPTIONAL HABITS
> • • •

We thought about our 4.0 GPA's and figured that whatever we had been doing up to that point in terms of time management must

have been effective for reaching our academic goals. Our solution—
We decided to wake up early enough to spend time with God, eat
breakfast, get dressed, *and* complete an hour of schoolwork before
our 10 a.m. class. We knew that our minds were most clear in the
morning, so working one hour later in the evenings was not a good
idea. (See "Maximizing 'Alert' Hours" below.) **It is also important
to be flexible, depending upon the state of your body.**

Some nights, we did feel alert enough to work one hour later, so we
did. In those instances, we slept that extra hour the next morning.
Other nights, we tried to stay up and work an extra hour, but ended
up dosing off in our books. When you are watching the back of your
eyelids just as much or more than your textbook, your productivity
is clearly reduced! Your time would be much better spent if you
took a break and started again, or if you chose a better time period
for your body. What we did in those times was simply get up and
get in the bed! Whatever we didn't finish, we woke up in enough
time to finish the next morning.

MAXIMIZING "ALERT" HOURS

Around nine or ten o'clock in the evening, do you experience any
of the following symptoms?

- Do your eyelids become heavy?
- Do you become distracted by thoughts of who is going
  to call you or what show is coming on?

- Do you become fidgety and restless?

If you answered "yes" to these questions, you are probably a daytime worker.

All of us must take note of when our minds are most clear and focused, and schedule most schoolwork (or anything of importance that requires keen thinking) during that time of day. **Whatever time of day that you are normally least distracted and most focused is the time that you should use in order to maximize your mental productivity.**

Other activities that require the use of motor skills, as well as leisure time activities, can be done during the time of day when you are less mentally productive. Of course, life demands that you use almost all waking hours of the day for mental labor. In that case, just make sure you are not sleep, distracted, or relaxing during your most productive hours. **Always seek to maximize your most productive hours of the day.**

MAXIMIZING THE MINUTES (TBC AND TRANSITIONS)

Want to know how you can find the time to work thoroughly and in a timely fashion to stay ahead on all of your assignments and not pull all-nighters?... **It is the time that others waste, and many don't even realize where it goes or how productive it *could* have**

been... What time is this?... Call it The Prosperous TBC—time between classes!

Your life will change when you begin to **utilize all time between classes.** Many waste the day by losing the hours between classes and waiting until night (when all classes are over) to begin their homework. Instead of going back to your room to take a nap, hanging in the hallway to chat with friends, taking extended lunch breaks, talking on the phone, and posting on social media, actually use the time between classes.

Use TBC to get a head start on assignments, reading, or studying that you already know you have to do. Remember, there is always something productive you could be doing. **All of the minutes in the day add up to hours, which add up to days either utilized or wasted**. A great quote says, "Success is found in the daily details." **TBC is a useful, yet often neglected detail.**

Imagine how much more you could accomplish if you utilized "transition" time in the day. When you arrive early for class (hopefully), it is wise to study material for that class even if you don't have a test. That way, you can answer the teacher's questions; ask relevant and helpful questions; and, most importantly, gradually and effectively learn the

• • •

ALL OF THE MINUTES IN THE DAY ADD UP TO HOURS, WHICH ADD UP TO DAYS EITHER UTILIZED OR WASTED

• • •

information. If you simply review your class notes during that time, you will be surprised by how much easier study time becomes because the information is very familiar to you.

In college, we carried most of our books and notes with us even if we didn't have that particular class that day. This practice allowed us to do work for those classes during our transition time. For example, let's say I arrive early to my sociology class, but the only upcoming assignment for this class is a research paper. If I have 15 minutes to spare in this transition time, the kind of research and brainpower that it takes to work on this paper is not practical for this time frame. However, if I have my math workbook with me, I can use this time to get three math problems totally completed. It may seem small, but several instances of this kind of strategic work will combine to relieve you of nighttime labor. It helps.

For us, this kind of time utilization meant that if we were on a bus with the glee club headed to a performance, we were in our books round trip. Also, when we arrived early for rehearsals or meeting times before performances, we were in our books. When we ate at the school restaurant and had to wait 20 minutes for our turkey burger or hot wings, we were in our books. As you can see, much of the time that others let pass them by in the day, we utilized! *That* is **detailed time management that yields more rest** (nights and weekends) **and greater success. Always value your time, and treat time as your treasure** (because it is!!!)!

CHALLENGE

1. Determine your short-term goals for your next long reading assignment, paper, etc. and what your corresponding incentives will be at those markers.

2. E.g. After writing two pages of my research paper, I will eat an apple and have a 10-minute phone conversation with my boo J.

3. Say "no" to the next time-consuming offer on a weekday.

4. Make a detailed to-do list with everything that is on your mind, and organize it based upon your priorities and deadlines.

5. Ponder what your most productive hours of the day are, and how to best utilize your TBC and "transition time" this coming week.

CHAPTER 4

*N*ERDY NUGGETS FOR 100%:

Study Tips that See Results

KEY: PREPARE FOR PERFECTION!

Electro was selling some ence fo' tha low on his <u>graph</u>—
<u>Electroencephalograph</u>! What a crazy, yet memorable way
to remember a long, unfamiliar term for school. We have
had many laughs over some silly-sounding sentences that we have
created to internalize a long or difficult word, connect a list of facts,
or remember any random piece of information.

ACRONYMS AND ASSOCIATIONS

Use acronyms to aid recall of facts. Even if it doesn't quite make
sense, it is memorable, and you will chuckle while acing the test!
For example, to remember the order of our flat key signatures in
Fundamentals of Music Theory, we created the following sentence:
a boy named **CiF** gave a **BEAD** to a **G**irl named **C**ourtney. We used

the list (**C, F, B, E**…) as an acronym and expanded it to form a memorable sentence. This sentence aided our recall of **C, F, B, E, A, D, G, C** in order. Because we had to know how many flats were in each key and since each key increased by one flat, knowing the order was extremely beneficial. We always had a system to figure out how many flats were in each key. For instance, C-0, F-1, B-flat-2, E-flat-3, A-flat-4… If we were asked how many flats are in G-flat, we would think, "…**BEAD** to a **G**irl named **C**ourtney…SIX!!!"

Even to remember the order of the old church modes in music theory… "**ID** gave a **PLuM** to **AL**" to recall **I**onian, **D**orian, **P**hrygian, **L**ydian, **M**ixolydian, **A**eolian, and **L**ocrian. Sometimes you have to purposefully arrange the items of a list into an order that you can make an at least halfway sensible sentence out of. *This is productive study time!* A common acronym used to remember the Great Lakes is **H.O.M.E.S.**—**H**uron, **O**ntario, **M**ichigan, **E**rie, and **S**uperior.

For a health and fitness class, we made associations to remember the six dimensions of wellness. We imagined an employee physically walking into work (his occupation), sitting down alone in a cubicle being anti-social, working using his intellectual side, crying because of his emotional loneliness, and finally, praying to get a spiritual high while at work. Now, you have a mental picture to remember the six dimensions of wellness—physical, occupational, social, intellectual, emotional, and spiritual.

Acronyms and associations help you to remember the order of information, which is an important element of memorization. Keeping a consistent order in your mind as you memorize lists, especially, helps prevent you from leaving out anything. Think about the example above: how can he jump to the spiritual act of praying without the emotional loneliness before it, since that emotion was his reason for praying (specifically, in this scenario)? Each building block to the story works with the other to help you keep order and remember all of the information.

Similarly, **making associations helps you to remember facts, such as names and dates in history books!** If you are studying Marco Polo, you can always read his name with an Asian accent to remind you of his association with China, and even if there weren't a swimming pool game named after him, you could make other associations. You might have a friend named Mark who you can imagine in a Polo shirt. The more associations you can connect into one picture, the better! Therefore, picture your friend Mark wearing a Polo shirt standing next to your twelve-year-old brother to remind you of the century Marco Polo was born.

To remember dates, let's use his birth and death dates as random examples (1254-1324). Either associate the numbers in couples or in directions. For example, use the couples 12, 54, 13, and 24 in interesting ways, or think "up one" (1 to 2), "down one" (5 to 4), "up two" (1 to 3), "up two" (two to four). Therefore, when you try to recall the number, you know what century you start with (your twelve-year old brother), and you know the interval and direction of increase between the numbers. Now you can test your memory with constant, identifiable factors.

Find as many anchor points as possible. These anchor points will help you if you begin to draw a blank during your exam. In the scenario listed above, if your mind goes blank about the year of Marco Polo's birth, one of your anchor points is your twelve-year-old brother, giving you the century. Also, when remembering dates in history, you *must* practice recalling them in relation to one another. Therefore, if you recall who was born in 1244, and you remember that you established that Marco Polo was born 10 years after him, you can't possibly write that Marco Polo was born in 1234! **Creating associations is key because they are your memory's anchors!**

• • •
*C*REATING ASSOCIATIONS IS KEY BECAUSE THEY ARE YOUR MEMORY'S ANCHORS!
• • •

You can even make crazy/memorable sentences out of word syllables in order to remember long words, like what was done with *electroencephalograph.* For example, we randomly looked up the term *asthenosphere* to see what strategy we would use to remember it. First, you must separate the syllables and use them to create small words. We see *as, then, o[r]* (Add what you need to make it work!), and *sphere*. Now you can link them together by making up a dumb sentence. For example, (threatening furiously with your index finger pointed and swinging) "You had betta fix my hair *as* you did *then or* I'ma throw this *sphere* (spear but sphere, get it?!) at you!!!" You and your study partner will have a great time laughing, but when it appears on the test, this sentence will come to mind, containing every element of the word. Hey, it worked for us! Don't knock it 'til you try it!

CLASS ATTENDANCE

"I can't wait to get to college so I can choose when I feel like going to class and when I don't. Nobody can tell me what to do, so I can just chill and do my homework and come to class to take my tests. People tell me that the teachers don't care anyway. After all, it's college!" –says the typical high school student.

Interestingly enough, class attendance is a common piece of the puzzle of school that students look forward to skipping in college. Truthfully, the teachers do care. Even if it's a large classroom setting and the professor doesn't notice you're missing, he/she *will* notice the students who are always there, on time, and sitting on the front row. This kind of active participation will help you excel in your classes. Also, you can't take advantage of this next study tip without going to class.

NOTE-TAKING

Always be prepared and alert to take extremely thorough notes in class. Let's avoid the "sick" a.k.a. "sleep" days and even the instances when people skip one class to prepare for another. All of this can be avoided by actually preparing for class in advance. Also, if you absolutely cannot be in class because of an unavoidable emergency, ask another attentive student who makes great grades and takes thorough notes to provide notes for you to copy. (Do not just ask a friend of yours!)

It is extremely important to have thorough notes! Some of the very details mentioned in the lecture might not be in the book but might appear as one of the questions on the test. It happens all the time! Teachers often highlight in class what information is important to them, even if the book does not deem it important. **At the end of the day, what was in bold print or italicized in your book will not help your grade if your teacher puts something totally different on the test.** With that in mind, if you don't come to class, you can only study what is emphasized in your book. When you have covered ALL grounds of given information for study, you can be confident that you have all of the material you need in preparation for that 100% versus just a "passing grade." Study all information given in class, including information given (verbally) in lectures, terms and concepts written on the board, worksheets, study guides, and even online resources.

USING RESOURCES

"Dang, that test was hard! I studied last night, but nothing in that 'fill in the blank section' was even in the book in bold print or italics! That teacher is trippin'. I know I did terribly."—An example of the kinds of comments we heard after a particular test we took in college.

There is a reason that the two of us seemed to be the only ones we knew of who made A's on this test. The teacher used information from online flashcards he had suggested that the class use to study for the exam. Some of the information on these flashcards was not in the book, lecture, or on the study guide. Each of this professor's tests contained some questions from these flashcards, and most people had no clue where the information came from and how we were expected to know it. Both of us, however, studied every resource the teacher provided, and, therefore, made 100% on many of our tests during this challenging course.

Most of the courses we took in college did not provide study guides as a resource for preparation. This factor did not hinder our success because we developed systems of study to cover and internalize all possible information for testing. These are the methods we are sharing in this chapter.

STUDY GUIDES

Note that whenever you are given a study guide that has terms and concepts on it, USE it. That means, make your own document that has all the terms and concepts included in the study guide. Take the time to look through your textbook and define or explain each term/concept on your own separate document. The teacher's study guide is only useful if you define everything to make your own detailed study guide. Also, typing the information will help you become familiar with the material in your study process. **Creating study guides is part of the memorization process**.

We cannot tell you of the many times we have done exceptionally well on tests that other students called difficult, simply because we utilized the study guide as described above. Sometimes, students are blown away by questions that are asked on tests, even when the hint to study that information was on the study guide. Although it seems obvious, it is repeatedly proven by students' behavior that we should emphasize to USE STUDY GUIDES.

READING

"Aww man, I didn't know my test tomorrow is over six whole chapters! I guess I'll have to skim through them as fast as I can in these next four hours until I have to get up and shower before class."

Reading is something that many students deem nonessential because they feel that they can "get by" without it…going to class, looking over the bold print terms at the last minute, and the like. The truth is, it is better to be safe than sorry.

Reading is a great safety net to give you ultimate comfort about your class material. When you have read along the way, regularly attended class, reviewed your class notes, utilized the study guide, and used any additional resources suggested by your professor, you can be confident that there will be no information required from you on the test that you have not already seen. There were many times when material has appeared on our tests that was not in bold print or in italics, but was simply found in the general reading. Without reading, you can "get by," but that will be all that you'll do. **Aiming for that 100% takes specificity and intentionality.**

Do not wait until the night before the test to read the chapters that will be on the test. Read your assigned material when it is assigned. Remember that active, engaged reading, which yields comprehension, is beneficial reading, not just scanning your eyes over words. Write your thoughts and questions about the reading and discuss it with your study partner or whomever you end up chatting with after you read. Also, read your class notes weekly to keep abreast on the

• • •

*A*IMING FOR THAT 100% TAKES SPECIFICITY AND INTENTIONALITY.

• • •

information. That way, when the quiz or exam approaches, it won't seem to you that you are seeing the information for the first time. You will be familiar with everything, and be on the second step to memorization (the first step—attending class, on time! The second step is reading!).

Before you read the designated chapters, **be intentional about the time of day you read**. Do not read after eating a heavy meal because you would have so much blood going forth for digestion that the blood flow to your brain would be decreased, and you would become sleepy (a condition otherwise known in some cultures as the infamous "itis"!). You need that blood flow to your brain for concentration. For your reading time, choose whatever time of day you are most alert: if you are more alert in the morning, read in the morning. Reading requires more clarity of mind than performing math problems, practicing music, or engaging in hands-on coursework.

When we read for school, we prayed and asked God to lead us to what we should underline or highlight. Try not to highlight excessively because then you will still hinder focus when looking at the page. If almost everything is emphasized, highlighting will lose its meaning. Also, underline only important words in each sentence. **Limit your emphasis to as little as you can underline and still comprehend the meaning when looking back on it later**. Generally, this means ignoring prepositions, articles, and some pronouns. After creating this focus in the textbook, you are prepared for study time whenever that approaches.

Sample underlining: <u>Freudian psychiatry</u> and extreme <u>environmentalism</u> in <u>early psychology</u> contributed to the idea that <u>parents shape</u> their <u>children's futures</u>.

STUDY BREAKS

"I've been studying all these notes, flashcards, and readings, and busting my brain to figure out what I can use to remember this junk for the past four hours! I feel like my brain is like the cheap paper towel brand on that commercial that is not absorbing this stuff anymore... Every few minutes, I have to purposefully re-open my eyelids because I realize I am dosing off. I go from *asthenosphere to Zzzz...*"

When you get sleepy or extremely restless while studying, the best thing to do is take a break. Otherwise, you will end up wasting more time by losing momentum and productivity. This could be a *strict* 10-minute phone conversation (Tell the person when you call that you only have 10 minutes. Maybe even set an alarm.). It could be a *light* snack break (10 minutes) to get an energy boost (notice light snack, as to avoid the notorious "itis"). Your break might need to be a 15-minute power nap.

How do you keep this nap from being your sleep for the night?

Set your alarm on the most annoying ringtone possible, and put it across the room on your dresser or floor. That way, you have to turn it off, and you have to get out of the bed in order to do so. It's dangerous to keep the alarm right next to your pillow when you know you're likely to roll over and turn it off without even thinking. Do not sleep inside of your bed, but rather on top of your comforter so that you don' t get too comfortable and refuse to get back up. If you have a sofa, nap on that instead. When you return to work, you will feel more refreshed, alert, and equipped to think than you did before.

SPACED STUDY

"Are you kidding me?!!!" What do you mean I got a 70 on this test? I studied for 6 hours last night!!!" said Andy. Adam responded, "I only studied two hours last night, and I made a 100 without any nerves. Want to know the secret?..."

When you have to study, it is much better to space your study time over more days/weeks so that you can internalize and review information free of stress. **It is proven that spaced study time is more effective for long-term retention than cramming.** Not only does this technique normally

• • •

*I*T IS PROVEN THAT SPACED STUDY TIME IS MORE EFFECTIVE FOR LONG-TERM RETENTION THAN CRAMMING

• • •

guarantee you confidence and accuracy when testing, but it also allows you to achieve the purpose of education in the first place—LEARNING!

Knowledge is power, and it adds value to us as individuals. Therefore, never lose sight of the importance of actually learning instead of only passing. Cramming might help you to pass, but not necessarily to learn. When you have your degree in hand, you want to be certain that you have the knowledge and skills to back it up. For whatever profession your degree is supposed to prepare you, you want to be as equipped as possible. At the end of the day, what matters is "What can you do?"! Greater knowledge and a broader skillset make you more competitive as a candidate, more confident as a student, and better at whatever you do.

For a moderate-length quiz, take two days to study the information. Study the underlined/highlighted information, study guide, and other provided resources the first day and review the same information the next. By the second day, you should test your memory by glancing at the page and then looking away to fill in the blank with the bold print/italicized terms. If you are working with a study partner, have that person quiz you on the important terms and concepts of the chapter.

When a more extensive exam approaches, take four to five days to do the same process with several chapters and all other provided resources for study. (See chapter 5, "How to Schedule Perfection,

Part I" under "Studying" for more details on how to schedule your spaced study for maximum preparation.)

We should always keep in mind the importance of effective study beyond the test. Even if the knowledge is unrelated to your profession, you never know when that might be the topic of discussion around people you want to impress! Take the necessary number of breaks to keep your mind fresh and focused, and space your study time over multiple days/weeks so that you focus on retention and mastery!

PRAYER IN THE PROCESS

"10...9...8... Aww man, in a matter of seconds, this chemistry test is about to be an epic fail! Lord, please help me to pass this test!"

Many religious students wait until right before the test or quiz to pray when they are nervous. What they need to know is this—**last minute prayer that isn't coupled with proper study is an overall waste of time** [Faith without works is dead! (according to James 2:17)]. On the flip side, **prayer before and during the process of studying** is very beneficial.

• • •
For US, PRAYER WAS A SIGNIFICANT PART OF THAT EXTRA ON THE ORDINARY TO MAKE AN EXTRAORDINARY STUDENT
• • •

What should be the first step to your study process is the one most often forgotten—prayer. We all have times when we feel like it's too hard to concentrate. We get distracted and sometimes have our minds so cluttered with life matters that it's difficult to focus on our work. Sometimes, our distractions are as simple as thinking about what we will do later in our free time, daydreaming about our special someone, or playing with our toes! No one is exempt from getting so tired that work becomes a blur. Although we know that we're in school, we often stay up too late talking to somebody or playing around. Getting enough sleep is a major plus, but it is often neglected. Sometimes, life just happens, and we have to make accommodations for that.

When you need a solution, pray. Prayer was part of our preparation in all that we did in school. As we've stated in many of our interviews and in regular conversations, we prayed before we did any kind of homework or reading, before we studied, before we worked on projects, and before quizzes and tests. We needed God to lead us to the material we should pay close attention to, to help us remain focused, to aid our brain's absorption of the information, and to speak to us concerning the best methods of study. **For us, prayer was a significant part of that extra on the ordinary to make an extraordinary student**.

CHALLENGE

1. Create a sentence to help you remember a long or difficult term and a date that you have to memorize.

2. Before your next big test, try spacing out your study time. Create a plan based upon how much material you need to cover and how many days you have to prepare. Also, keep in mind to space it in relation to the workload you have in other classes.

3. For your next long span of study time, take breaks. Try different things for your break time to see what works best for you (e.g. talking on the phone, eating a snack, taking a nap). Avoid what you find to be addictive!

4. The next time you have an upcoming test, pray before you study. **Sample**: God, please help me to focus on and retain all of the information that will be on this test. Please give me energy, clarity of mind, and divine strategy as I study. Help my score to be 100% on this test. Thank You! In Jesus' name, amen.

CHAPTER 5

HOW TO SCHEDULE PERFECTION,

Part I

KEY: PLAN THE PARTICULARS FOR UNBEATABLE PREPARATION.

Freshman year for Jamie began with a great deal of stress. Although she was told in August, the beginning of the semester, about a test in political science that was scheduled for October, she did not study for it until the day before the test! You might be thinking that this doesn't sound so bad. Unfortunately, she did not realize until the day before the poly sci. test that she would have to study for a history quiz also! Because Jamie didn't read the syllabus or remember the history quiz, she was forced to stay up until 6 a.m. trying to study more than a month's worth of material for the poly sci. test, and trying to memorize two chapters' facts for the history quiz.

Her test was at 9 a.m., and her quiz was at 10 a.m. After she stayed up all night, which happened to be the third time that month, she felt a sore throat coming on, a runny nose leaking furiously, and a throbbing headache. Because Jamie got sick, she stayed in bed the next two days and then had only Thursday to cram a paper for Friday. She ended up with a C on the poly sci. exam, a C- on the history quiz, a B- on the paper, four absences from her classes, and a weekend shut inside to recuperate for the next-go-round. What a way to begin college! Unfortunately, scenarios such as this one often occur in school because the average student does not know the art of scheduling.

Although scheduling sounds boring and meticulous, it actually leads to things we all want! Who doesn't enjoy sufficient sleep, good health, regular meal times, and time to relax? What about undisturbed time to spend in peaceful devotion with God? And who can refuse having time to work on your passion *in addition* to having time to work towards top-notch grades? Scheduling can help you achieve all of these desired objectives.

Once you determine what your priorities are, schedule them so that they are guaranteed attention in your day. We should all make daily schedules for all activities, including schoolwork, work, and fun on the weekends! It is particularly important to schedule EVERYTHING you value getting done during the weekdays.

We should have some things on the schedule weeks or months in advance, such as assignments that require long preparation. **We**

should make weekly and daily schedules! Every Monday (or Friday before) of every week and whenever you receive assignments, schedule what days and what hours you will use to complete those assignments. Often, the further in advance something is scheduled, the more efficiently it will be prepared. Nevertheless, **the daily details are**

> *• • •*
> *ONCE YOU*
> DETERMINE WHAT
> YOUR PRIORITIES
> ARE, SCHEDULE
> THEM SO THAT THEY
> ARE GUARANTEED
> ATTENTION IN YOUR
> DAY
> *• • •*

what truly make the progress. Therefore, this chapter will discuss how to schedule your daily and long-term priorities.

LARGE ASSIGNMENTS & PAPERS

"What are ya'll working on? I can't believe ya'll are starting on that paper already! I'm in the same class, and I haven't even touched that. And for what? It's not due til' two weeks from now. (Two weeks later…) That teacher is stupid! I can't believe she gave me a D on that great paper I stayed up all night working on! What did ya'll make?"—This is the kind of chatter we heard many times when practicing what we're preaching now. The following will explain why we made A's on the largest, most challenging assignments in college.

For long assignments and/or those that are worth a large percentage of your grade, plan to start several weeks in advance in order to work most efficiently. For example, when you are assigned a long paper, schedule to begin writing it as soon as possible. Complete it at least a week ahead of the deadline to allow time to edit it daily, with a clear mind, so that you submit your best product.

Early completion is accomplished by starting the paper at least 2-3 weeks before the due date and allotting certain hours per day to edit it. Make sure you choose longer spans of preparation time (2-3 hours, no less than 1 hour) versus shorter increments (30 minutes). We say this because this kind of assignment requires focus and a "train of thought" that sometimes takes a while to turn on. It is more difficult to restart your train of thought than to continue. Use your shorter increments of time in the day for math exercises, reading assignments, etc.

• • •

*I*T IS BETTER TO READ A PAPER EVERY DAY FOR A WEEK, GRADUALLY REVISING IT DAY BY DAY, THAN TO READ IT TWENTY TIMES IN ONE DAY AND SUBMIT IT BY MIDNIGHT!

• • •

Finishing your long/weighty paper or project a week before the deadline will also grant you enough time to take your paper to the writing center at your school (We definitely took advantage of this freshman year!) and to gain feedback from friends/ family members who are great writers.

Working on these assignments early

and extensively simply yields opportunity for better results. The more time you use to improve the paper after writing the rough draft, the more organized, polished, and error-free the paper will be. **Just as spaced study time is most effective for retention, distributed editing allows you to identify much more clearly what needs improvement and to develop the best solutions. It is better to read a paper every day for a week, gradually revising it day by day, than to read it twenty times in one day and submit it by midnight!** When you proofread a paper every day, you will notice more mistakes, and you will have an opportunity to improve it each day. Try it, and you'll see!

STUDYING

Jasmine had a 40-question quiz over 5 chapters in her world religion class. She studied, but only the night before with her Red Bull, Snickers bar, and cup of coffee in hand. Although she might have been able to *recognize* the information and pass a multiple choice quiz with an average grade, this quiz was composed of all fill-in-the-blank or completion questions. She wrote "I don't know" or "I'm not sure" on many of the questions on this quiz. The lesson— **distributed study must be practiced for long-term memory and recall capabilities.**

You should ALWAYS plan in advance how many days or weeks you need to study for something before the assignment is due or the test is given. This time varies depending on the magnitude of the assignment/quiz/test/exam.

If it is a small quiz, meaning one that encompasses 1-2 chapters, you should allot at least 2 days BEFORE the day of (I must specify on that one, whew!). This means that if the quiz is Thursday, thoroughly study *all* of the materials Tuesday and Wednesday. On Thursday, you review to lock it in and see everything one last time.

If you are preparing for a test that covers material for 2-3 weeks, you should follow the procedure for quizzes, but add a day. **The more nervous you are about being tested, the earlier you should start studying. Spaced and extensive studying breeds retention and confidence.**

If you are preparing for a midterm or final exam, you should begin preparing 7-10 days prior and study the material daily. You will need to divide the material into a feasible and comprehensive schedule. For instance, we might study chapters 1-5 on Monday, 6-10 on Tuesday, 11-15 on Wednesday, etc. **Make sure you divide the material in such a way that you can study all of the chapters thoroughly at least twice before your final review.** That means that once you have studied all the chapters, you have enough days to start again. For example, Thursday, study chapters 1-5; Friday, 6-10, etc.

• • •
*S*PACED AND
EXTENSIVE STUDYING
BREEDS RETENTION
AND CONFIDENCE
• • •

The final review should take place the day before and the day of, either skimming through underlined material (ALL) or reviewing the major concepts from self-made study guides or other resources. Making these kinds of study schedules at least 2 weeks in advance is always necessary.

Whatever final papers or projects that are due during the same time should be completed early, if possible, so that you have more focused study time before the exam. Otherwise, you will have to intensely study for multiple classes at the same time that the paper or project is due.

Notice that the schedule for midterms and finals is always predictable because you *know* you have large tasks for each class that are due at the same time. Therefore, whatever you can finish early (besides studying), get it out of the way, and then make the appropriate study schedule for *each* class. There are certain papers and projects you are aware of in advance. You can easily lighten your load for later by completing these early. Because time is limited, note which classes need more (or less) repetition (days) of study than others in an effort to schedule accordingly.

GROUP PROJECTS

Don't we all hate group projects! You are forced to depend on other people for the success of your grade, and you have to be inconvenienced to work around other students' schedules. There are always people who have to make up for the slack of other students in the group. There is always something annoying and unfair that arises when working with groups.

Unfortunately, these kinds of encounters occur in life in general while working with a team. Wherever there are people, there are problems. Period. With the "glass as half full" perspective, wherever there are people, there are opportunities. **The more minds that are present, the greater the diversity of ideas, creativity, and skill sets that are available.**

For example, during our freshman year, we had to create a performance project for the midterm in our African Diaspora and the World class (ADW). Our project wowed the class, the teacher, and ourselves! Even the dean came to see our group project because her interest was piqued when she saw us preparing on the campus.

One group member wrote our skit content in the form of an astounding spoken word piece. For effect, another group member played her clarinet for the piece's background music. The two of us wrote a relevant song to sing, choreographed a dance to a pertinent song for the group to perform, and helped with content and the beginning of the spoken word format. All of us working together made a much better project than we could have done alone!

That project did not become great over night, though. We met many weeks, probably even a month in advance. We met 2-3 hours at a time and sometimes multiple times a week. Although not all group projects require this amount of time and intensity, proper scheduling will eliminate unnecessary stress and produce the best product.

Group projects need to be scheduled for early completion and spaced completion. Otherwise, they can become a real monster and a serious burden! Because of the likelihood of encountering lazy, nonchalant, or procrastinating people in one or more of your group projects, you should assume the leadership role. As soon as you know who your group members are, get all contact information. Schedule *at least one meeting per week* or create one assignment for each member to complete weekly until the project is completed. You should schedule to complete it at least one entire week before the due date.

The reason you should schedule weekly progress meetings is that coordination of different students' schedules around their classes, projects, and extracurricular activities can be a major hassle. Therefore, waiting until the last minute to meet would create the need for multiple meetings in the same week, which might not be possible for all members. If it is absolutely necessary, you might have to meet Saturdays or Sundays. Nevertheless, beginning far in advance, plan to meet at least once a week, on weekdays, so that you won't have to interrupt your weekend and cram meetings, risking that some team members still won't show up.

If the midterm or final exam is the group project, use that as an incentive for the group and tell them that the goal is to finish it before the hectic study time for exams. Tell them that since everyone will get busier around that time, it only makes sense to complete the group project during the calmer time of the semester. **Be the one to send reminders and inquire about everyone's progress. Set deadlines for them to meet along the way** to make sure that procrastination will not cause a poor, rushed product at the end. Remember that you don't know what your group members' skill set is, and you might have to correct their work so that your grade does not suffer. If you are not grammar-savvy or skilled in that particular subject, you might need to ask another trustworthy group member to review everyone's work. Either way, you need everyone's portion of the assignment in advance!

• • •
*W*ORKING AHEAD YIELDS LESS STRESS AND OFTEN YIELDS BETTER QUALITY WORK
• • •

When scheduling the completion of your assignments, plan to begin the large ones early enough to have plenty of time to successfully complete those that require much more time, even when you are assigned other small tasks along the way. Always avoid the student's/the employee's/the ambitious dreamer's great foe—*procrastination!* **Working ahead yields less stress and often yields better quality work.**

GROUP PROJECTS BONUS: HOW TO LEAD YOUR GROUP TO VICTORY

When rising as the leader of group projects, remember to be as likeable as possible while still acting as an effective leader. If you throw your weight around, make demands, tell peers "what to do," allow your frustration and annoyance to show, and bug your group members about deadlines, they will either respond to you with a bad attitude or not at all. There is always a right way to say what needs to be said. In reality, you *are* "telling them what to do" and assuming responsibility for the project. However, they don't need to *feel* like you are!

Be smart about the way you lead. Ask yourself the question, "Would I feel disrespected or annoyed if someone approached me this way?" Treat others with respect, even if they act like irresponsible slackers. After all, that could have been you before reading this book! ☺

Use terms like *we* and *let's*, rather than *you*. For example, "Hey ya'll! Let's meet on Mondays after class. Does that work for everybody? Let's also divide the content six ways and bring our research to our next meeting."

Additionally, when delegating tasks for the project, make sure that the project responsibilities are divided according to the skill sets/

strengths of the individuals in your group so that the work is of optimum quality.

Also, regularly solicit their input so that they know that they are valued and included in the process. They might have something great to offer that you didn't think of. If they have a bad idea, just say, "Okay, umm... I was thinking something more like... What do you think about that?" They will likely agree with your better idea. You can also make them feel like their bad idea was incorporated into the chosen strategy ("The new one is 'our' idea!") by saying, "Oh okay, that idea gets me thinking about... What if we use this portion of your idea but with this spin on it...?"

Another possible outcome when asking your group's input is that they might have nothing at all. Then share all of your ideas after all. That way, they can never say you were unfair or domineering! It is, however, important to always encourage them to bring their own ideas to the table so that all team members participate in the process.

Try brainstorming sessions. You can ask everyone to come up with a certain number of ideas, and you can put them in a hat anonymously or write them down to form a list. Then the group can evaluate the options, vote on the best, or even combine some of the ideas to formulate the best outcome. Make sure that, if the brainstorming is done verbally, the quiet and passive members give their ideas first. It is counterproductive to allow their ideas to be influenced by the outgoing members. Remember, when brainstorming, the more ideas, the better! You never know when one little idea can spark a masterpiece!

When you check on your group's progress, try something like this: "Hey Sam! I hope your week is going well and that you aced that psychology test you told me about ☺. Have you gotten a chance to finish section four of the biology project yet?" If the individual says no… "Okay, well can you get it done by tomorrow at 5?" They say, "Okay, I guess I can do that…" You respond, "Great! I'll add it in as soon as you send it! Our group will be so relieved to finish this project more than a week before midterms! That way, we can focus on our other classes, since we know we're all *swamped*! (chuckle, chuckle) Thanks, and have a great day!"

Keep in mind to assert your leadership in a friendly, likeable way that doesn't make your peers feel like you're trying to be their teacher or boss. **When they like you and respect you, they are more likely to cooperate with you.**

ACADEMIC GOAL-SETTING

"Failure to plan is a plan for failure," as our dad often says. If we don't set daily, weekly, and monthly academic goals to support our plan of action, we will more than likely not be as prepared, balanced, and successful as we could be.

We should always read the syllabus for each class and determine which months and weeks we need to begin preparing for large assignments. Refer to "Large Assignments & Papers" section above to get an idea of how you need to prepare for those assignments, and set your monthly goals accordingly.

Where the rubber meets the road are the weekly goals that are achieved by accomplishing daily goals. Establish a goal for each course per week and then plan which hours and which days during the week you will achieve those goals.

Sample:

Academic Goals to Complete by Friday of This Week:

- Write paper for English class
  - Monday: Finish research for paper
    3-5 p.m. and 8-11 p.m.
  - Tuesday: Complete outline and rough draft of first 2 pages
    10-11:30 a.m., 1-2:45 p.m., and 7-9 p.m.
  - Wednesday: Complete pages 3-6
    3-5 p.m. and 8-11 p.m.

(You get the point. Plan so that you know you will finish the entire paper by Friday, leaving next week for editing.)

- Study for human anatomy exam
  - Monday: Study chapters 5-7
    10-11 a.m., 12-2 p.m., and 7-8 p.m.

- Tuesday: Study chapters 8-11
  11-12 noon and 6-8 p.m.

(Remember that the goal is to have studied all of the chapters by Friday so that you can review the same chapters next week.)

***You should repeat this process of deciding your attainable goals for each course for the week, and then plan which hours of each day you will use to make measurable and pre-determined progress.

To plan these schedules efficiently, you should look at the clock so you know how long it takes you to finish various academic tasks. For example, how long does it take you to read 10 pages of your history book with a clear, refreshed mind? How long does it normally take you if you are tired? About how long does it take you to study a chapter in your psychology book? How long does it take you to write one page of a research paper? How long does it take you to complete 10 algebra problems?

Once you have established how long it takes you to complete various tasks, your schedule can be accurate. **Always allot more time than needed versus just enough or too little.** Therefore, if you happen to get interrupted, you still have time to meet your goals for the day. If you finish early, GREAT! Move on to the next task early. By the end of your day, you have great options: (1) work ahead for tomorrow, (2) treat yourself to recreation time, or (3) get additional precious sleep!

PARTICULARS

"I thought I was going to have a whole hour to study before my 3 p.m. class, but I guess I forgot about the 20 minutes it would take me to get to school from home, *plus* the extra 15 minutes waiting in traffic, *and* the 45 minutes it would take me to pick up my lunch and eat it. Aww man, this is messed up! I guess, at this point, what I make is just what I make on this quiz."

It might seem overboard to schedule your days just this meticulously, but <u>the more accurate and practical your schedule is, the more efficient it is</u>. When you make your daily/weekly schedule, you must factor in all time in the day so that there are no surprises. If you schedule what you will do with every hour of the daytime, but you only consider your class schedule, you will be unpleasantly surprised at how much less time you have than what you thought.

Always overestimate how much time you will spend on everything, including travel time. This means driving to and from campus, walking from class to class, dorm to class, to lunch, and to other places. When you factor in travel time with a little cushion for traffic and/or conversation while going from place to place, you will have a more accurate idea of how much time you actually have for your schoolwork.

Also, factor in lunchtime when scheduling your working hours. Even if you eat while working, you will work more slowly. There might also be conversation during mealtime, which will certainly delay the process. It is great to unwind a bit and truly enjoy your lunchtime, but you should always put a time cap on it and follow it strictly except in cases of emergencies. If you brought a lunch, 30 minutes will suffice for your lunchtime. If you are eating on campus, 45 minutes should be fine, and if you are eating off campus, one hour should be allotted.

Sample: A day in your scheduled weekday life…

Monday

6:00 a.m.- Brush my teeth, make the bed, use the restroom

6:15 a.m.- Pray

6:40 a.m.- Read the Bible

7:10 a.m.- Eat breakfast

7:30 a.m.- Shower and dress

8:15 a.m.- Go to school

8:45 a.m.- Complete a few math problems or study biology notes while waiting for class to start

9:00 a.m.- Biology class begins

9:50 a.m.- Go to the restroom and go to the computer lab

10:00 a.m.- Study for psychology test

11:40 a.m.- Walk to music theory class

11:55 a.m.- Study music theory notes while waiting

12:00 noon- Music theory class begins

12:50 p.m.- Walk to computer lab

1:00 p.m.- Write pages 2-5 for ADW research paper

4:45 p.m.- Go to glee club rehearsal

5:00 p.m.- Rehearsal begins

6:30 p.m.- Get dinner (+travel time)

7:30 p.m.- Read English literature

9:30 p.m.- Take a break

9:40 p.m.- Study for theater quiz

10:15 p.m.- Talk on the phone

11:00 p.m.- Get precious sleep!

CHALLENGE

1. Look at your syllabi to see what papers, projects, group projects, and exams you should begin weeks in advance. Mark on your calendar when you will begin each large assignment.

2. Practice distributed study by studying for your next quiz/test far enough in advance so that you have time to study the same material AGAIN. The key is to make sure that this second study session occurs on a different day than your first study session on the same material.

3. Establish goals for each subject for the week, then plan which hours and which days during the week you will achieve those goals.

CHAPTER 6

*H*OW TO SCHEDULE PERFECTION,

Part II

KEY: PROVE THAT YOU VALUE IT BY SCHEDULING IT.

"Wow, with all of the time I put into the glee club, you would think I was a glee club major, if such a thing existed! Funny thing, I'm just a music major with a vocal concentration who has glee club as a *life* concentration!"

EXTRACURRICULAR ACTIVITIES

Extracurricular activities are great for relaxation and even for your resume, especially when you are in leadership roles of organizations. Nevertheless, we must always prioritize education. For us, the glee club was an extracurricular activity that was required in order to complete our major. We were committed members of the Spelman

College Glee Club from first semester of freshman year until our last semester of senior year.

This organization was extremely time consuming, as we had three rehearsals a week for 1 ½ - 2 hours each, 2 sectionals a week for an hour each (until we became section leaders, which resulted in an increase to 4-5 sectionals a week), tours (1 ½- 2 weeks long), and performances on week days and weekends throughout the school year. We had even more rehearsals during the semester as we prepared for our Christmas Carol Concert (which happens to be the weekend right before final exams). In addition to rehearsals and sectionals, we had to practice with our sheet music and pianos separately in order to master the repertoire throughout the school year.

In the end, the amazing experiences, relationships, funny stories, and skills that we developed through the glee club made all the time and hard work worth it! We planned our assignments and studying around glee club obligations, doing everything in advance and taking materials with us when we traveled.

A vital lesson—Do not over-commit yourself! We didn't volunteer for extra involvement unless we knew for sure that we had the time to offer without slacking on work or our precious sleep. Therefore, if you decide to participate in extracurricular activities, choose something that will be worth your while and then plan your schedule accordingly!

A girl named Karen was really gifted as a dancer and wanted to be a professional ballerina. She was part of a liturgical dance ministry at her church, and she was also involved in the swim team at her school. When she became busy with the swim team, she became unfaithful to the dance ministry. Her mistake in this instance was allowing herself to be so busy with more than one extra-curricular activity that she was unable to be committed to her schoolwork, swimming, and dancing. Her number one priority needed to be her academic work! Dancing should have been next on the list and then her swim team commitments after that.

It is important to have your extra-curricular activities in line with what you desire for your future, in some capacity. It does not have to be directly related. For example, if you want to do something with public speaking in the future, you can invest your time in a debate team. Although a debate team is not directly related to motivational speaking, it is complementary because it offers oral training and helps you to think quickly and spontaneously.

Our heavy involvement and leadership in the Spelman College Glee Club improved our ears for vocal blend, intonation, advanced vocal technique, and use of dynamics and articulation. It also increased our knowledge of how to work with vocal ensembles. Since completing our college education, we apply all of those skills as we lead the youth choir and praise team at our church. Time is far too precious to waste it on activities that are just for fun instead of activities/organizations that are enjoyable and beneficial to your development. Let your extra-curricular activities be strategically related to some aspect of your future.

RECREATION

There are two reasons that it is extremely wise to schedule your fun or wind-down time. First of all, if you don't, you might be on the road to a nervous breakdown! Having some way to wind down at the end of the day, whether you have a great phone conversation, listen to uplifting music, play your favorite game or sport, pray, read the Bible, etc., helps you to relax and be rejuvenated.

On the weekends, you should always have something either fun (Clean fun is the best fun!) or relaxing to look forward to. Spending time with funny friends at the mall, movies, a restaurant, game night, movie night, etc. can be a great stress-reliever. If you aren't a social butterfly, your relax time during the weekend could include just sitting on the couch watching TV (Avoid excess of anything!), reading an entertaining book, or playing video games.

We almost went crazy during freshman year when we thought it was a good idea to study the entire weekend every week! When we learned that we must enjoy the journey and use wisdom by scheduling our recreation time, our journey became much sweeter, and we retained our academic success.

The second reason for scheduling your recreation and relaxation time is to prevent you from deviating from your work and other priorities. For instance, when you get a phone call during the week while you are doing your work, you might stop and have an hour-long conversation. Afterwards, you might be so tired that you are less productive than what you would have been if you had taken the phone call at a designated time. This designated time would be during a much-needed break (less than 1-hour, of course) or when you have finished your scheduled work for the night. If you made the mistake of taking a long, unplanned evening break, you might keep working and work more slowly or quit before finishing the amount you originally planned to complete.

If you schedule to stop studying at 9:00 p.m. to talk on the phone until 10:00 p.m. and then head off to sleep, the phone call will not serve as a distraction or hindrance. Instead, it will serve as an incentive, giving you something to look forward to at the end of the day. More importantly, it can serve as an evening wind-down to get your mind off the worries of the day.

PRECIOUS SLEEP

Ahh, one of the most soothing parts of the day (besides meal time)—bedtime! During this part of the day, every care of the day can be replaced by "z's," and every muscle in your body can relax, releasing all tension. Your immune system is repaired, your mind is cleared (unless you have a nightmare!), and your breathing is slow and deep, flowing needed oxygen throughout your body. When your eyeballs kiss the back of your eyelids, and your head snuggles with your pillow for this one-of-a-kind date, what a wonderful experience!

Believe it or not, sleep is important. Adequate rest is needed so that you can be most efficient during your daytime hours. Although people's bodies are different, teenagers generally need 8 ½-9 ½ hours of sleep each night, and adults need 7-9 hours. Additionally, consistency is key to being most alert throughout the day. You should aim to wake up at the same time daily for best results. Sleeping too long can cause drowsiness also. Even concerning naps, you should keep power naps under 45 minutes to avoid interrupting your deep sleep time frame. **If your mind isn't clear because you are drowsy, your rate of productivity declines.**

In addition, **sleep deprivation weakens the immune system,** making it easier to get sick. Sickness can certainly hinder productivity. Think about it! Even the common cold can cause you to waste time. When you experience coughing spells while in quiet time for study or reading, you must pause to collect yourself because you cannot focus while coughing repeatedly. Of course, this wasted time adds up.

Also, when you have a runny nose, you have to constantly stop your schoolwork to get tissue and wipe your nose! How annoying! No one likes being sick, and the truth is, the time spent coughing, wiping your nose, making tea, sleeping excessively, visiting the doctor, and going to buy cough drops could be better spent in many other ways.

When you schedule your time in such a way that you are ahead in your schoolwork, the notorious "all-nighter" in college can be unfamiliar to you! You can actually schedule what time to go to sleep when the assignment is not due TOMORROW!

You should evaluate your progress on your assignments and calculate the remaining hours that you will have to work on the assignment in relation to the time you will need for other projects/study that week.

• • •

*R*EMAIN AHEAD, SO YOU CAN GET IN THE BED!

• • •

Always remember to **remain ahead, so you can get in the bed!**

YOUR GIFTS

You should also schedule time to work on your primary gift(s) that is (are) vital to your destiny. After all, when you graduate, the world will want to know what you can do well, not just what you know. A wise man once said (mi padre, btw), that practice may not make perfect, but "practice makes better."

If you are gifted with computers, for example, the more you operate them, the sharper your gift becomes. Although you will, at some points, encounter technical problems that you may not know how to fix, you will improve. Since we are humans, we should become comfortable with the reality that we will never be perfect. **New target—Progress, not perfection!**

For some reason, there are students who major in disciplines that do not coincide with their gifts and passion. They select majors based upon family pressure or how much money they think they will make after graduation. This kind of decision often leads to a miserable college experience and is not recommended! You do not want to end up in a career that you hate, dreading every Monday because you have to start another week at work. Time is too precious, and so are you and your God-given talents.

One day, you will probably decide to switch to something you love anyway. Therefore, you might as well sharpen your skills in the field of your passion. That way, you can be excellent at what you love to do. Think about it! People were given different talents and desires for a reason. Operate in YOURS, not someone else's.

If you do, however, find yourself in a major that is not your passion, make sure that you create the space in your schedule to improve your skills in your area of passion. After all, you do want to be ready for whatever opportunity is in your future for you to dive into your passion full-time. For example, you might be a philosophy major with a dream to be a famous dancer. Make time to watch other famous dancers on YouTube and practice your craft regularly.

That way, when it is time to audition for Juilliard, you are excited and ready!

If you aspire to do a profession you find difficult to know how to prepare for in your spare time, use people and books. If you know someone who does or has done what you desire to

> • • •
>
> *If* YOU DON'T KNOW HOW TO GET TO WHERE YOU WANT TO BE, READ THE LIFE STORY OF SOMEONE WHO DID!
>
> • • •

do, find out how you can communicate with him/her. Make that person your new mentor, if possible. If mentorship isn't possible, schedule whatever you can with the individual, whether a lunch date, phone call, or email conversation.

If you don't personally know of someone who is an inspiration in your desired field, locate biographies of those examples. Read, read, and read some more! **If you don't know how to get to where you want to be, read the life story of someone who did!**

DEVOTIONS

Spending time with God daily in devotion is the best and most significant priority. It is the most refreshing, inspiring, fulfilling, and moving part of the day. During this time, every care in life fades into the background while God is the center of attention.

During this time of prayer, listening, reflecting, and reading the

Bible, we are rejuvenated spiritually, mentally, and emotionally, which often transfers to physical energy as well. Christ deserves first place in all of our lives. Not just because we are "suppose to" spend time with Him, but because He loves us and we love Him. When you love someone, you want to make time to spend with him/her, right? Anything less will cause the relationship to suffer because of the distractions and busyness of life.

Relationships are the essence of life, and our relationship with God is the most important one! When planning what time to get up and get ready for the day, we simply schedule extra time to spend time with God. Some others prefer evening or mid-day. Whenever you are least distracted is the time you should select for your daily devotion time with God. However, for consistency and reliability, set a time to keep daily that cannot be interrupted by other events. This will eliminate the "I ran out of time because…" excuse.

CHALLENGE

1. Evaluate your extracurricular activities and other weekly commitments. Are you spending major time in activities that will not be useful to your career/destiny? Which extracurricular activity is most helpful and enjoyable?

2. Evaluate your sleeping habits. Are you often drowsy during the day, unfocused, or sick? How many hours of sleep do you get?

If you do not get sufficient sleep currently, what will you do to gain more?

3. What practices do you currently incorporate or will you initiate to sharpen your skills in preparation for your future career?

4. How much time will you designate for your devotions daily? At what time?

COMPREHENSIVE CHALLENGE (PARTS I&II)

1. Including each component of scheduling (section titles) from "How to Schedule Perfection" Parts I&II (Chapters 5&6), write in order what you will do tomorrow from the time you wake up until the time you get your precious sleep. Be as detailed as possible.

   - What time will you wake up tomorrow, after all your snoozing, if you tend to utilize that button?

   - How long will you spend in prayer and Bible reading/study?

   - How long is your breakfast time (that is, if you value the most important meal of the day that will energize you for your morning class and help you burn more calories throughout the day... J)?

   - How long will it take you to get ready (shower, fix your hair, etc.)?

- How long will it take you to get from your dorm to class, or from home to school and from the car to your classroom?
- What will you study in the gap between your first two classes? What are your study/homework goals for the entire day (to make progress on your week's goals)?
- ETC.

2. Make sure your schedule for the week is accurate so that you can have more recreation on the weekend! Whatever you don't finish during the week, you must plan for the weekend. If this happens, which you should try to avoid, schedule what you will do for fun and the hours you will spend doing that activity. Include who you will spend time with as well, making worthy investments!

CHAPTER 7

CONNECTIONS THAT BOOST GPA:

Maintaining Helpful Relationships

KEY: PEOPLE CAN PROPEL OR PREVENT YOUR SUCCESS.

We have all seen society's portrayal of a teacher's pet. This person sits on the front row of class everyday, always raises his/her hand to ask and answer questions, and expresses great interest in the class topics. Some people might call it a suck-up, but we call it the hook-up! Winning the hearts and earning the respect of teachers and other authority figures in your life are critical to your success. Authority figures in your life, as well as friends and study partners, can aid or hinder your success.

TEACHERS: HURT OR HELP

"If you're sweet, I'll do what I can to help you. If you have a bad attitude, it will not go well for you." This is a paraphrase of what one of our professors told our class on the first day in our first semester of freshman year. He told us that professors can help you or hurt you. He then proceeded to tell us stories concerning this principle. He explained that he learned this principle in college and graduate school, and that he now observes it in operation among his colleagues and even himself.

This professor told us that, because one of his professors (when he was a student) was late coming to class one day, the whole class left (except him), as is customary according to students' 10-minute or 15-minute rule, depending upon the professor's degree status. Basically, if you have "Dr." in front of your name, you get a 15-minute grace period until the students escape as quickly as possible before the teacher shows up! Well, when the professor arrived, this man was the only one still there, waiting for his arrival. The professor felt highly disrespected by those who left on the one day that he had a set back, but he felt very pleased by the one student who stayed. Therefore, when grades were returned, he only had mercy on the one student who stayed, and he failed every other student in the class.

Our professor went on to tell us that his colleagues actually discuss their students by name among one another, meaning that students' reputations from class to class precede them. He said that some professors are less merciful toward students who have a reputation of being lazy, irresponsible, or disrespectful. Our professor told us that he is the same way. He said that if you are nice to him, he will help you succeed, as all teachers do (just without telling you upfront), but if you have a nasty attitude, what you get is what you get!

Even after he explained this to us, some students were still disrespectful and irresponsible. Of course, when they needed mercy or another opportunity to turn in an assignment, he responded—"F." As for those who conducted themselves better, he helped them with the concepts after class and even switched the percentages of certain assignments in the final calculations to improve their grade. For example, let's say I made a 95 on my paper that was worth 10% of my grade, and I made a 70 on a project that was worth 20% of my grade. In this instance, the teacher might make my 95 worth 20% of my grade and the 70 worth 10% of my grade. What a pleasant trade for having a great attitude! (If you were wondering, yes, we did earn our grades. We are referring to others who needed switched percentages. ☺)

If you still don't believe us, at a different school, the same results were proven. This student was in violation of principle 13 in "How to Win Your Teacher's Heart", which you will soon read below… In his religion class, Corey debated his teacher, repeatedly voicing all of his disagreements about the teacher's opinions concerning doctrine. He made all A's in the course, but his final grade was an A-! Why? Because, the teacher was insulted and thought the student was not open to learning.

With a different teacher, a similar situation occurred. Corey's whole team clearly conducted better research and gave a better oral presentation in front of the class. The other team even rated his team better! The teacher gave Corey's team a worse grade and lowered many of his other grades because he had a poor relationship with her. By the end of the course, although he did better than other students and the grades were always curved, he received worse grades. His friend's work was the same as his, and she received an A- in the course, while he received a B-.

In contrast, when Corey did not argue with one of his teachers, but instead nurtured a positive relationship, the teacher helped him. When he studied hard for a test and did not have enough time to finish, the teacher showed him mercy. He decided to change the percentages for him so that his better grades were worth a greater percentage of his overall grade than his poorer grades.

Whether the discrimination is as blatant as this or not, **teachers always have the option of giving you partial or no credit on certain answers and even have liberty when grading your papers**. They can choose whether they require an exact answer or one that is the general idea. For instance, let's say on your biology test the answer for #15 is *superior vena cava*. You wrote *vena cava*. Technically, you did not give the exact answer because it wasn't specific enough. You wrote so broadly that it could be interpreted as the whole thing, or even the inferior vena cava. Thus, if #15 is worth 10 points, your teacher has the liberty to mark your answer as wrong, or give you 5 points for it. These decisions are often influenced by relationships. Papers are also graded by the teacher's discretion. Through a lens of "This lazy student gets on my nerves" or "This negative student is always so disrespectful," the paper's content might not look as good to that teacher as the content of the respectful, attentive, diligent student's paper. Therefore, even on the most basic level of grades, relationships matter.

How to Win Your Teacher's Heart

Whether a teacher is lenient or strict, every teacher is impressed by a student who works hard and expresses interest in his/her subject.

• • •
*T*EACHERS ARE HUMAN, TOO
• • •

Even strict teachers might give you tips on how to better succeed on the assignments in the course. It is true that just as you would want someone to show interest in what you are saying and investing your time and energy in, teachers appreciate the same. **Teachers are human, too.** When carefully used by the student, the following tips are sure to develop and maintain a good relationship between the student and professor:

1. Pray for favor with your professors!
2. Sit on the front row in class.

3. Stay awake and look pleasant during class. Refrain from getting into a comfortable sleeping position!

4. Don't talk to your classmates during class.

5. Be early everyday.

6. Submit work early.

7. Ask questions frequently about course content [WITH knowledge of assigned readings and discussions!]. For questions that don't benefit the entire class, i.e. regarding personal difficulty you are having with an assignment, ask after class or before class to avoid wasting lesson time.

8. Ask for help with papers and assignments long before they are due.

9. Greet the teacher upon entering and exiting the class.

10. Be cordial when passing the professor in the hallways or anywhere else outside of the classroom.

11. Email papers for advance (1-2 weeks) teacher feedback (if that teacher allows).

12. Ask professors for detailed preferences regarding how assignments should be completed.

13. Avoid arguments with the teacher. Be respectful and calm when expressing opinions in class, particularly on the subjects of religion, politics, or any other topic involving much passion or controversy. When heated debates arise in class, resist the temptation to participate, if possible.

14. Avoid complaining to the teacher or to other students

about the teacher's decisions.

15. Only submit your best work, meaning you have edited and revised it before submission. NO TYPOS.

16. Apply the same amount of effort to every assignment, regardless of the percentage of your grade it is worth. **Make quality your policy.**

17. **Always go the extra mile!**

GOING THE EXTRA MILE

Going the extra mile means that you do more than what is required of you on assignments and other requirements that don't even

• • •
*M*AKE QUALITY
YOUR POLICY
• • •

receive grades. For instance, two different teachers asked us two consecutive years to participate in research day to represent our academic department. We did not want to participate since it was not required, and we knew that those kinds of projects would require a lot of additional preparation time. Nevertheless, we were honored that they asked us, and we decided to grant the professors' request, just to make them happy. You should always take advantage of opportunities to work with teachers and be intentional about maintaining excellent professional relationships with them.

A similar experience of ours not only involved a sacrifice of time, but precious time on a Saturday morning when we could have enjoyed sleep! Our fitness teacher wanted the class to participate in the school's 5k walk/run early on a Saturday morning. He said, "If you come to this event, you will not have to attend the following class." When he saw us at the race, he said, with a very pleasant smile and tone of voice, "I'm not surprised to see you girls here." He said this because we had created a "go the extra mile" kind of reputation for ourselves. And guess what? We also attended the following class, which was not mandatory due to our participation in the run. As expected, many others did not attend class that day. Again, he affectionately said that he figured we would be there, because "You two always are."

We were early to every class and were often the last to leave the workout room, while others usually left early. We were participatory, turning in work early, and asking a lot of questions about details of what he required for upcoming assignments. These actions caused us to stand out in our teacher's eyes.

Because we missed the first day of class due to the glee club's performances in Washington, D. C., and we were late for the second class because our car battery died that morning, it seemed as though this teacher was not fond of us initially. He displayed some strange facial expressions that proved to us that he had the wrong idea about our character as students and our work ethic. This bothered us a bit, but we knew that we would soon show him otherwise. Throughout our college experience, we always prayed for favor with our teachers. As a result [of our faith + works], God turned this teacher's heart towards us after all. He later began to identify us as exceptional students who fulfill all requirements and exceed expectations.

Never missing a beat is another benefit of going the extra mile. Although we were exempt from attending the class period after the 5k walk/run, the professor still gave lecture notes that were not in the book but that were on the test the following week. If we had not gone to class that day, we might not have made A's on that test.

Going the extra mile in our classes helped create a reputation for ourselves of respectability and even trust between us and our teachers. Here are some perfect examples: 1) During freshman year, our car was stolen. Naturally, we missed our first class that day, but we called for a ride to avoid missing the rest of our classes. 2) When we totaled our car right in front of school, we were extremely late for class (Yes, we did still run to class! We told you we were serious students…). Our teachers did not ask us for police reports even though attendance was mandatory. They said that when they noticed our absence, they knew that it must have been an emergency, because we were always in class. These instances touched our hearts. From such experiences, we knew that we had gained the respect of some of our strictest teachers and that God had answered our prayers for favor!

BIRDS OF A FEATHER...

"Birds of a feather not only flock together, but they also fly to the same destination." This means relationships influence mindset, which influences behavior, then lifestyle. Because you become more like those who you are close to, your actions begin to resemble theirs. These actions determine the direction of your life. This principle is important to note for your friendships regarding every aspect of your life. This even includes your academics. **Your friends can aid or hinder your success.**

It is extremely helpful to have friends who motivate you to succeed because they are such hard workers themselves. Surrounding yourself with people who expand your thinking and make you feel uncomfortable in laziness helps to push you to do more. For us, that person was each other. Some people said that we were the ones who motivated them to do better in school because they saw us studying all the time. It made them think, "Maybe I should be doing my homework…"

The opposite is also true. Spending time with people who do not spend adequate time studying can distract you from being productive and can make you feel comfortable slacking. It is interesting to note how often students are looking for other students to validate their laziness as normal. For example, one student will ask other students, "Hey, have you started studying for this test?" or "Have you done this assignment yet?" Typically, the students laugh together as one admits in a nonchalant tone, "Nah, I haven't." Then another says, "Me neither!" and so forth. The more students who say they have not done what is expected, the more comfortable each student feels, and the laughs and laziness are multiplied! This behavior can build camaraderie among students while simultaneously deteriorating the value of a strong work ethic.

STUDY PARTNERS

Extremely focused study partners can also provide camaraderie, but in a more constructive sense. Now make sure you use your noggin when choosing a study partner. Choose someone who is already excelling academically, someone who is already focused. **Do not expect undisciplined people to, all of a sudden, become productive when you study with them**. If they are not successful themselves, they cannot help you to reach your goals. Focused study partners provide motivation and discipline, making you feel uncomfortable with laziness. They drive you toward productivity and sharpen the part of you that desires to succeed.

• • •

*D*O NOT EXPECT UNDISCIPLINED PEOPLE TO, ALL OF A SUDDEN, BECOME PRODUCTIVE WHEN YOU STUDY WITH THEM

• • •

When you stay up late studying together, choose to consume an energy drink for the first time (We never did! ☺), or nudge each other when dosing off after having a long week, you form a supportive and encouraging relationship that helps you succeed academically with less stress. When you laugh at bags under each others eyes, laugh at one another getting silly after it gets late, and take food or nap breaks together, you create memories that make your relationships even more enriching! **You should apply wisdom to your choice of friends in life so that they are people that motivate you toward daily discipline and propel you in the direction of your destiny.**

CHALLENGE

1. In the list under "How to Win Your Teacher's Heart", choose 3 of the principles that are most challenging for you and try implementing those first, starting this week. You can always begin anew by being punctual, attentive, and friendly in class this week, and turning in your assignment early!

2. Examine the habits of your friends and how you feel when you're around them. Pray and choose your circle wisely.

3. Find the best student you know or know of in your respective classes, show yourself friendly, and ask him/her to be your study partner.

CHAPTER 8

HOW ROSE-COLORED GLASSES CHANGE EVERYTHING:

The Power of Perspective

KEY: PAINT YOUR LIFE PORTRAIT THROUGH PURPOSEFUL PERSPECTIVE.

S arah: "Hey Brandy, how are you?"

Brandy: "I'm really not doing well at all. My boyfriend just broke up with me three weeks ago, and it feels like my world is crumbling. He was my best friend, boyfriend, joy, and my light. Without him, everything looks so dark, and I can't imagine life without him. That's 3 years down the drain."

Sarah: "Man, that is so crazy! My boyfriend broke up with me last week! And we'd been together for 4 years. Honestly, I've been doing all right. I think it might be a blessing in disguise… We'd been so focused on each other that I don't think we'd really been focused on our careers the way we should have been. With the way I've come to see it, at least I can get more sleep, focus on my professional goals, and spend more time with friends and family. After all, romance isn't all there is to life."

Brandy: "Wow Sarah, I can't believe you're smiling right now when all of this is still fresh. Good for you, but I want my man back!"

The power of perspective… This story demonstrates how the same situation can look hopeful or hopeless depending on the way you think. **The ability to use your thoughts to shape your world is a powerful tool.** Now, let's think about it more deeply.

Life is actually not what you see, but how you see it. Our mom taught us a long time ago the value of looking at life through rose-colored glasses. She said, "If you look at the sky through dark shades, regardless of what the sky truly looks like, you will perceive your surroundings as dark; but, if you look at the sky through rose-colored glasses, you will perceive a rose-colored world!" Such is life. Your attitude and mindset, which we call perspective, will determine the way you view people, relationships, problems, opportunities, and life in its entirety. **The way you view the situations of life will determine how you respond in those situations.**

• • •
*L*IFE IS ACTUALLY NOT WHAT YOU SEE, BUT HOW YOU SEE IT
• • •

For example, you could view an

opportunity to study abroad as a long, scary time to be homesick and possibly fail, or you could view it as an amazing opportunity to see the world, meet new people, and explore a different culture. If you view it the first way, you probably won't take advantage of the opportunity. It's true: the way you respond to opportunities and to obstacles in life can determine your success or failure.

You could view change as something to fear or as an adventure to embrace and explore. If you choose the first one, you could miss out on promotion, development, and eventful stories to tell. Now, what about obstacles? One way to view an obstacle is as something that is in your way, keeping you from moving ahead. You could embrace that definition or choose another one instead! An obstacle can alternately be viewed as something that causes you to develop a more creative and character-building strategy in order to move forward. Which perspective of obstacles do you think will take you further in life?

MIND GAMES

"I love this class, I love this class! This is my favorite textbook, and I am so excited about this test!" These are sample words from a student who makes C's and D's in this particular class of his/her weakness, but is striving toward progress. There was actually a successful lawyer who came to our freshman-year English class to share this insight with us. She said that she hated one of her classes in college so much that she looked at the textbook with dread and, therefore, never wanted to read it! **She later realized that if she wanted her grades to improve, her attitude had to improve first**.

What was her solution? She started telling her textbook that she loved it every time she saw it. She repeatedly confessed that she loved the class and the book, even though she did not. She probably began by saying it in a joking and sarcastic way, but she continued. She admitted that soon after, she began to feel better about the book and the class. Gradually, she lost her dread and disgust for the course. As her mindset about the course changed, so did her grades! She ended up with a final grade that she was extremely excited about and proud of. She used this story to demonstrate how a purposefully positive and driven perspective propelled her to arrive to her current career and life success.

Some call it "positive confession," and others say it's "speaking what you want into the atmosphere." The Bible calls it "the power of the tongue." Sometimes you have to tell your mind the opposite of what you feel. **If you can convince yourself that you love something you currently hate, your emotions are bound to follow your new way of thinking**. The Bible discusses "[calling] those things which are not as though they were" (Rom. 4:17). This means that it is not yet true, but you want to see it true in your future. <u>You speak what you want, not what you have.</u>

Many students repeatedly make negative statements such as, "I

HATE this class," "I HATE my teacher," or "I am about to fail this test!" **When you speak or think negative thoughts, even if you feel that they are true, then you feed those negative emotions and you prepare your mind to have that negative experience. In reality, your words and thoughts attract that negative experience!** Think about it. Someone who hates something or believes that he/she will fail at it will not try as hard as the positive thinker because he/she is expecting a negative result. However, when you tell yourself something positive that isn't true, but you want it to be true, you can cause your mind to view the situation more positively. **When your mind changes, your actions follow, and so do your results.**

Once your perspective changes, you view your obstacles as challenges that you are excited to conquer, versus dreaded barriers that doom you to failure. If you can convince yourself that you love your worst class, you will have a better attitude about your schoolwork, and you will work harder in it. Why? Because you believe that it is possible for you to excel. With this perspective, you *expect* to excel, and you discipline your mind and actions to do what is necessary to achieve your goals.

Also, remember to accept your academic weakness just enough to change it, so that you are motivated

• • •
*W*HEN YOUR MIND CHANGES, YOUR ACTIONS FOLLOW, AND SO DO YOUR RESULTS
• • •

to work harder. Avoid repeatedly declaring and convincing yourself that you are weak in certain areas. **The words of your mouth can be the product of your perspective, or you can use your words to influence your perspective.** If you say something enough, you will start believing it. After you believe it, your perspective will change. Again, when your perspective changes, your actions will change with it.

Think about it! If you are told daily that you are fat, even if it is not true, you might start believing it. Next thing you know, you are pinching your stomach and eating less at the dinner table. You might even say to yourself, "Dang, I am getting a little flabby." Just as the negative words that you say and hear impact your perspective and behavior, so do the positive words.

> • • •
> *WHATEVER YOU CHOOSE TO FOCUS ON WILL BE AS IF IT WERE PLACED UNDER A MAGNIFYING GLASS!*
> • • •

Whatever you choose to focus on will be as if it were placed under a magnifying glass! Ever wonder why the more you talk about a bad situation, the more negative thoughts come to your mind, and the angrier you become? The list gets longer and longer, and before you know it, nothing looks positive! The individual looks like a complete villain, you look like the victim, and the situation looks hopeless. Your academic situation can even seem impossible. You start believing the teacher doesn't like you and is determined to make you fail, or you say to yourself, "I'm just not cut out for school!" These scenarios are evidence of the effects of focus.

MAGNETIC FOCUS

The way to maintain a proper perspective is to be *intentional* in your choice of how to view the situations of life. **Don't let your views be created by your circumstances!** We noticed a significant difference in our attitude in college when we gained a different perspective of the glee club. We used to be extremely frustrated in rehearsal when it would continue past the designated time frame, and no one was allowed to leave. Because we were very organized, we had already planned the time we would complete our assignments after dinner, which was after glee club rehearsal. Of course, when our schedule was removed from our control in that way, we became stressed.

Initially, we viewed the organization as a group that we were forced to be a part of that constantly swallowed our time against our will. Every time we were required to attend a last-minute performance, buy something for performance wardrobe, meet an hour earlier (than we were scheduled) to leave for an off-campus engagement, or stay overtime at rehearsals, our attitudes were poor. We almost viewed each requirement as a punishment. However, when our perspective about the glee club changed, we began to appreciate the great opportunities the glee club provided and the importance of the relationships we were able to develop.

We began to prepare mentally, for whatever happened, to avoid becoming frustrated in unfavorable circumstances. We also decided to maximize the waiting time by always having some of our homework with us. We allowed God to use the glee club to help us develop patience and to learn how to be flexible. When we made the choice to view the organization as something of value instead of something to dread, our experiences became much more positive. The following saying is true: **negative attitudes draw negative experiences**.

When our perspective is negative toward a particular circumstance, the root of the problem is focusing on all of the bad. Using our example with the glee club, we were at first focusing on the following: (1) last-minute performances, (2) rude and annoying upperclassmen, (3) extended rehearsals (that weren't specified in the syllabus), (4) early call times, and (5) traditions concerning freshman students that made us feel like the rookies.

To be intentional about the way you view your circumstances, create a "positive" list. When we decided to change our perspective, we focused on the following: (1) bringing inspiration and joy to others through music, (2) encountering celebrities (e.g. singing back-up for

NEGATIVE ATTITUDES DRAW NEGATIVE EXPERIENCES

Aretha Franklin and opening for John Legend), (3) belonging to a special sisterhood, (4) creating hilarious memories with other freshmen during our first year together, and (5) growing musically in ways that voice lessons alone couldn't provide. We cannot emphasize enough the importance of the following, so we will say it again: **write a list of every positive element of your circumstance and focus on that every time you get frustrated or angry.**

Your focus acts as a magnet. Here is a quirky example of the way that focusing on fear can serve as a magnet for undesirable occurrences: Our grandmother once told us that people attract their fears to themselves. The day after she shared this with us, we, along with some of our cousins, experienced its truth during a strange and scary encounter with a water bug (flying roach!) in our uncle's SUV. As impacting as that situation was for us as pre-teens, we experienced a much greater example during our freshman year of college.

Since the start of our first semester, we feared the possibility of our car getting stolen from our condo near campus (because of its location). During our second semester, that is exactly what happened! We were headed to our 9 a.m. class, and we were shocked to discover that our car was no longer in its parking space. We immediately began praying, and we walked all the way around the

• • •

Your FOCUS ACTS AS A MAGNET

• • •

building, hoping that the thief hadn't made it far, and we'd find it parked on another side. To our dismay, it wasn't there.

We cried a little, called the police, and then began discussing, between the two of us, ways to view the situation differently. We said, "Even though all of our books, class notes, GPS, video camera (that had our group project on it), clothes, and shoes were taken with the car, our sole purpose on this earth is to live for God." We knew that we could definitely do that without all of those items. Even if we flunked out of school because we had no books or notes during the last few weeks of school before finals (although that clearly wasn't His will), then we could still live for Him, share our faith, and He would work everything out for our good (Romans 8:28) and His glory. After this mental shift, we actually saw a reason to smile and laugh before the police even arrived.

We soon had another reason to laugh when we called our mom, and her prayer included "...let that thief's buns be ON FIRE until he brings the car back!" We were cracking up, and she was actually serious! To this day, she does not remember that prayer, but we believe God answered it because the car was found at the end of the week with many of the thief's belongings still in the vehicle (although he was never arrested). Really, who would abandon a car with their stuff still in it? Our friend's theory was that the "buns of fire" was diarrhea, which caused the man to run into a restroom at a store in the plaza where the car was found!

HOW PERSPECTIVE PAYS

After our initial shock about the car theft, we changed our perspective. We prayed, believed, and experienced uncommon peace for the circumstance. We believe that if we had allowed ourselves to have a pity party, complain, and cry out of hopelessness and anger, we would have never pushed to pray and smile in the midst of it all. Without prayer, the car may have never been found, and we would have never received all of our class notes before final exams. Additionally, when the car was found, we decided to focus on the class notes that remained in the vehicle, instead of on the rest of the material possessions that were stolen from the car (the GPS, clothes, shoes, video camera, etc.).

We also decided to concentrate on the love that we felt from other students and even faculty. When we needed books and transportation, we found that people actually cared about us! A young lady in the glee club gave us expensive textbooks for a class we were taking (She had already taken the class.). We had a glee club performance coming up, and we realized that the black heels we needed were also in the stolen car. The glee club wardrobe mistress sent a text to the whole organization asking who had some shoes we could borrow in the correct sizes. We never forgot the generosity of our glee sisters who loaned us shoes without hesitation. Why look at the glass as half empty when you can view it as half full? **Concentrating on loss is never an effective tool of**

life restoration or improvement.

GRATITUDE

Gratitude is a particular perspective that makes each experience more bearable, hopeful, and joyful. With gratitude at the forefront of your mind and heart, there is no room for complaining, pity parties, or depression. Allowing negative attitudes to populate your mind promotes a selfish view of life. It's unhealthy to dwell on thoughts such as, "Why does stuff like this always happen to ME? Why can't MY life be easier like others I know?"

When you focus on gratitude, you spend your time and thoughts thanking God and others, not thinking about YOU. Also, when you participate in ministry outreach programs and community service, you will find it easier to maintain a grateful attitude. Once again, it removes the focus from self. When you begin to focus on the less fortunate and concentrate on how you can help others, you learn to appreciate your own life. **Use gratitude as your "rose-colored glasses" with which to view your life and the world around you.**

LIFE-CHANGING PERSPECTIVE PRACTICE

"Lord, I thank You for my hearing, the use of my vocal chords, my ability to walk, my eyelashes, hair, skin, safety, family, food, freedom, relationships, fingers, toes, education…" And the list goes on and on, but you get the picture. This is an example of shifting to the gratitude perspective. We call this the "counting your blessings" exercise.

A long time ago when one of us (Kristie) was going through a very emotional time of life, crying almost daily, easily angered and frustrated, a challenge arose. Her challenge was to count her blessings each time she was tempted to focus on the negative circumstances. When provoked to anger, it was EXTREMELY difficult to come to the point of even starting the exercise, but it actually worked! Once you make a decision to try it, you have completed the hardest part.

Start naming anything and everything you can think of, no matter how big or small. You can include the weather, your taste buds, your ability to breathe, talk, and walk, anything! The point is, we must be grateful for every blessing, no matter how "big" or "small." We thank God for our eyelashes (something others may consider small), knowing that it would be a huge deal if we didn't have them! Naturally, we didn't think about this until we saw a person on a talk show who never had eyelashes. She said that not having eyelashes is frustrating daily because dust, dirt, and lint constantly get in her eyes. If she could change anything about her life, it would probably be her lack of eyelashes, something most of us take for granted.

We ALL have numerous things to be grateful for, even though in the midst of negativity, we tend not to acknowledge them. When you count your blessings, expand your list until your attitude transforms. No matter how long it takes you to reach your breaking point, keep going! By doing this exercise, you will eventually reach a point at which you realize that you had been acting like a selfish child who wanted everything to go your way and pouted when it did not. As if your parent didn't just buy you a toy yesterday…!

By the time I (Kristie) reached my breaking point, I was crying and apologizing to God for my self-centeredness and my ungratefulness. I realized that I had much more to be grateful for than to complain about. **The list of blessings will ALWAYS outweigh the list of complaints.** When we realized how powerful this exercise was, we decided to continue its use, and we still do it today.

This exercise is so effective that it works for depression, also! There was a lady suffering from depression who heard of this gratitude exercise. She wrote a list of things she was grateful for. To her surprise, her list exceeded 1,000 items! She was so astonished at the number of blessings she already possessed, that it shifted her perspective of her life.

Of course, this one-time exercise does not shift your mindset forever. That's why you must repeat it when needed! This lady read her list of 1,000 items every time she began to sink into her downward spiral of negativity. She was able to maintain an intentional grateful attitude, and this perspective positively impacted her responses to the situations she encountered daily.

Many students (including us for a while) constantly complain about school—all the work, all the requirements, the teachers, the expenses, and all that they don't understand. "Why do we really need this class/assignment?" students often ask one another rhetorically.

Our attitude about school shifted when we realized just how many people around the world and in America only dream of acquiring a college education. To them, it is a prized opportunity that they hope for. To us, it is a burden that we complain about. For some it is, "Wow! I *get* to go!" For others, it is, "Dang! I have to go." How will your attitude towards school and life shift if you choose to focus on all of the positives versus the inconveniences and stresses?

CHALLENGE

1. Think of your most dreaded class or teacher this semester. Write a note (sticky note) to stick on the front of your textbook and notebook for the class that says, "I love this class! This is my favorite class!" If your teacher is the problem, the note should read, "I love this teacher! She/He is my favorite teacher!"

2. Identify the greatest challenge/obstacle in your life, currently. Write a list of opportunities that it presents. What attitude and action can you take to provoke improvement in your character and/or your situation? Write your plan of action and pursue it.

3. What do you hate the most about school? Write a list of positive elements about that factor. What can you gain either now or in your future: either personally (your character development) or professionally (your skill enhancement)?

4. The next time you become irritated, angry, or frustrated, pray about it and read the list of positives or the list of opportunities you have created. If it is something you cannot change, change your mindset by repeatedly telling yourself, "I love him/her/it!"

5. Write a list of all of your blessings concerning your education, as well as your life. Read it (out loud) the next time you are tempted to complain. A significant shift occurs when you hear yourself read it aloud.

CHAPTER 9

Making Average Your Enemy:

Committing to Excellence

Key: Perspiration + Passion= Preeminence

The notorious slacker—who hasn't met one of these?! "Shoot, I'll be happy if I can just pass this class! I'm just trying to do what I have to do to make it through, just cross that finish line, and I'll be good to go!" Many students think this way, even if they don't voice these thoughts. They are only concerned with doing enough to get by...to pass...but not necessarily to excel... This thought pattern is a precursor of mediocrity, as the student prepares, and, in fact, plans to settle for achieving less than his/her best. "Man, I was 20 minutes late for my 8 a.m. again. Normally, I am just too tired, and frankly don't feel like getting up on time...so I don't!" In order to be an exceptional student, you must be committed to excellence. **"Half-doing" things should be a foreign concept to you.** It should never be an option!

PERSPIRATION—HARD WORK

When you are committed to excellence, you do not have to be the smartest to eventually excel above those around you. It's great when people are genius in certain areas, but you can succeed without being a genius. **When you add diligence to passion, you can create something powerful and unusual.** This passion could be one for a particular skill or talent you are working to improve, for a certain subject or major of interest in preparation for your life dream, or simply for doing your best to achieve excellence in all that you do.

Some Americans assume that many high-achieving Asians are geniuses. The truth is, their culture demands a stronger work ethic. We learned about this first-hand during our first visit to Asia.

In the fall of 2013, we had the experience of a lifetime in Singapore! We tried native cuisine, traveled through the Night Safari zoo, shopped at many of the jaw-dropping malls, took pictures galore in the billion-dollar botanical gardens, formed meaningful relationships, and fell in love with the Heart of God Church.

• • •
*W*HEN YOU ADD DILIGENCE TO PASSION, YOU CAN CREATE SOMETHING POWERFUL AND UNUSUAL
• • •

While we were in Singapore to sing and speak at a conference at the Heart of God Church, we had a blast spending time with the people there and learning about their culture. We were told about the sometimes-burdensome pressure that Asian parents place upon their children to excel academically. For them, the highest achievement in your youth is to make straight A's through school, graduate and go to a top school of your choice, and then make a lot of money! Of course, these values sound similar to American values. The difference is subtle: Americans tend to value the same except for the heavy emphasis on being at the top of your class. American culture often focuses on graduation, while Asian culture aims for top performance before graduation. You notice people's real values by what they refuse to tolerate and by what they unwaveringly enforce.

Many Americans can learn from this culture the difference in performance when you roll up your sleeves, work hard, and aim to be your best. Of course, we do not endorse harsh, unbalanced application of this principle. Those that are extremely hard workers must also utilize proper strategy and maintain balance for holistic success. Now, let's take a look at an example of work ethic versus genius in our story.

When we were freshmen at Spelman College, we took a piano class so that we could pass the three required piano proficiency tests for our music major. The curriculum required that each music major (vocalists and instrumentalists) pass all three of the tests before the end of sophomore year. Like typical students, the first thing we did was complained! "Why in the world do we need to learn to play the piano when we are not piano majors? What does that have to do with singing? All we would need to do in life is just get a piano accompanist. This is such a waste of time."

After we finished complaining, we directed our thoughts to what to do next. Although we grew up with a piano in our home for most of our lives, we never learned to play the piano because we lacked the inspiration for it. Consequently, regret filled our minds on the first day of piano class…

Our fingers felt extremely awkward even forming a simple chord. We also had never learned to read sheet music for singing or for piano. We had previously learned all of our vocal parts in music by ear. While others came into class already reading music and knowing some basics of playing piano, we felt very behind. Because this was our first semester, we still had not adjusted to our busy schedule in college. What a rough start to college piano!

At the beginning of the semester, the instructor explained to the class that because this was a basic-level course, only five to ten minutes of practice a day was necessary to excel on the exams. However, in response to our self-imposed nervousness and urgency to meet our standard, we practiced playing piano and sight-reading sheet music for an hour a day, throughout the entire semester. In addition to this intense practice, we prayed about our progress and our grades in this class, as we always did for classes. While other students didn't even practice those five minutes, we did what we knew was necessary for our own development.

THE PAY-OFF

On the days that our regular piano quizzes were administered, we watched many of the other students wait until a few minutes before the teacher arrived to practice the particular piece of music for that week. We also observed many of the students stumbling excessively while playing through the pieces. The instructor stated that she could tell the difference between the kinds of mistakes students make when they have practiced and when they haven't.

When we took our quizzes and tests, although we rarely performed perfectly, the teacher was pleased with our performances. She knew that we had practiced, and she soon learned that we were hard workers. In fact, the instructor became frustrated with several of the other students who entered the class with more skill than we had, and their grades were not so pretty... In contrast, she distributed many A's to the both of us. These were not mercy A's, but *earned* A's.

We ended up being some of the top students in this basic piano course, while others struggled because of their lack of preparation. We made high A's at the end of the course and completed all three levels of the piano proficiency test by the end of our first semester of sophomore year. Remember, all three were not required to be done until the end of the second semester of sophomore year. Talk about being committed to excellence! ☺

Some of the same students who took the piano class with us did not finish their piano proficiency tests until junior or senior year. This taught us a valuable lesson our first semester of college: **We learned that the initial skill level or lack thereof does not determine the final outcome. It's about work ethic combined with prayer and faith.**

INSPIRATION FOR EXCELLENCE

"Why are you still doing schoolwork and it's Saturday afternoon?" "Why are you practicing for an hour and a half?" "Why are you waking up an hour earlier to do homework before your 10 a.m. class?"

• • •
*A*S YOU STRIVE TO REMAIN FOCUSED IN ORDER TO COMPLETE TOP-NOTCH WORK, YOU MUST HAVE A CLEAR UNDERSTANDING OF THE "WHY" BEHIND IT ALL—YOUR INSPIRATION
• • •

As you strive to remain focused in order to complete top-notch work, you must have a clear understanding of the "why" behind it all—your inspiration. When people come to you telling you that you're "doing too much" or that your extra effort isn't necessary, you have to know in your heart why it's important to you. In fact, writing down your motivating factors can help you stay focused and not waiver in your commitment to achieve your goals.

Examples of motivating factors:

> To learn important tools for my future
>
> To be the best in whatever I do
>
> To get/keep a scholarship
>
> To please God
>
> To meet my personal standards
>
> To make my parents and grandparents proud
>
> To get into grad school
>
> To create a remarkable reputation for myself as a student

Everyone should keep in mind his/her motivation. One of our greatest motivations is to do all that we do to the glory of God (I Cor. 10:31). Your motivation must be greater than what others are able to see or understand. They might observe your going the extra mile in school, at work, in random acts of kindness, and more, and be jealous of or annoyed by you because they think you're "doing the most." They might also be intimidated by the remarkable results you produce. Other people will not always understand your inspiration, but never allow their insecurities to discourage you.

People will always attempt to pull you to their level of commitment to school, God, and the like, simply because it's more comfortable for them. **Truthfully, it is sometimes better to conceal the details**

of your diligence to avoid the negative input of others.

In school, when other students in our class found out how early we began particular assignments, their response was not always one of admiration. They sometimes displayed jealousy and made comments such as, "Why are ya'll working on that already? I've got that same class, and I haven't even started." Comments like these were said with a tone that revealed their intention—to discourage us from starting so early! This was done to make them feel more comfortable procrastinating and waiting until the last minute to do their work.

• • •

*T*RUTHFULLY, IT IS SOMETIMES BETTER TO CONCEAL THE DETAILS OF YOUR DILIGENCE TO AVOID THE NEGATIVE INPUT OF OTHERS

• • •

Sometimes, people might try to make you feel stupid by saying, "You really need to start that early? I can knock that out in one day!" Well of course they can, but what will the teacher think about the assignment is the question…? Often, students act over-confident or too relaxed about schoolwork, but keep in mind that their standards/goals might be different from yours. They might be excited about a B or even a C in some cases, but you are always *preparing* for the A (the 100% to be exact). This is why your grades usually surface as superior. You have to discard others' negative opinions and focus on doing your best with God's help, as you apply all of the wisdom you receive from this book ☺. After all, a more efficient process, including diligence and pacing, yields better quality results.

A GOOD NAME, AN OPEN DOOR

"Are you serious?! You want *us*, inexperienced freshmen, to sing with the advanced chamber singers in the special spring concert, only weeks away?!"

It was our reputation of excellence in all that we did that caused our music director to propel us into greater opportunities. We were only freshmen in our second semester, and we were placed in the exclusive singing ensemble that was composed of junior and senior music majors. We were only in Music Theory I!

Nevertheless, because we made all A's in our courses, worked hard to learn our music for glee club, and always arrived early to rehearsals and classes, the director thought he could trust us. He knew that, regardless of how much time we would have to practice this difficult music (on our own) in order to catch up with the experienced sight-singers, we would do it. He was right! We worked our behinds off to learn that music as best we could before we were featured in the AUC concert with the orchestra!

When you operate in excellence, you will automatically create a reputation that brings you favor in the sight of peers, professors, deans, and leaders of your extracurricular activities. The Bible says that a good name is rather to be chosen than great riches (Prov. 22:1), and this is true. Because God does so much through people, your connections and relationships with people are important factors that can provide you with opportunities you could have never attained on your own. In school, you need your professors to think highly of you so that they encourage you to grow, show mercy when you need it, and recommend you for schools, internships, prestigious organizations, and more.

The same reputation of excellence that you develop academically can draw people to you at work and in other settings. Because people admire and reward excellence, you will gain respect and greater opportunities. You will be called upon as the person your boss can always count on to get the job done right and on time. Accordingly, your name will come up when an exciting opportunity/promotion becomes available. When you achieve academic or career success and carry yourself with respect and radiant joy, you draw people to you. As people come to you, you have open ears for whatever you want to share with them.

You can share advice and encouragement, and you will have a positive influence on those around you. If you serve God, you can choose to share your faith with others, because He is the source of your wisdom, strength, talents, and

> • • •
> *L*IVE IN EXCELLENCE, AND SHARE YOUR SECRET WITH OTHERS
> • • •

success. This is a form of letting your light shine before men so they may see your good works and glorify your Father, which is in Heaven (Matt. 5:16).

Live in excellence, and share your secret with others.

CHALLENGE

1. Examine your work ethic. Do you think the current state of your work ethic will help you achieve academic excellence, obtain your desired future career, gain admittance to prestigious graduate schools, or sharpen your primary talents?

2. For the next three days, apply more effort (time and focus) to your work than ever before. Note the difference between your new level of effort and your old habits, as well as the corresponding results.

3. Examine your motivation for school, work, extracurricular activities, etc. Create a clear statement of the "why" behind all of your work.

4. Operate in excellence!

CHAPTER 10

$\mathcal{K}$NOWING WHEN TO SAY YES:

Embracing Worthy Risks

KEY: PURPOSEFULLY SEIZE PRECIOUS OPPORTUNITIES.

Why do so many people love thriller movies? The good ones get your adrenaline pumping and have you on the edge of your seat in exhilarating anticipation of what will happen next! However, there could be a down side to watching a good thriller movie. You might experience tension in your body and maybe even nervousness, if you're the type to be stirred to that degree by a film. After it is over, you might be searching for the nearest friend who can give a good neck massage! Nevertheless, you enjoyed the movie. Do you ever wonder why we love roller coasters, despite the fear of falling out or getting stuck? What about horseback riding, skydiving, or bungee jumping? Each of these great adventures is connected to possibilities such as falling off, parachute dysfunction, or chords snapping. Yet, for some odd reason, many people find these activities worth the risk.

GREAT OPPORTUNITY, GREAT RISK

The greatest opportunities in life involve taking risks! Some of the riskiest activities enrich our lives with memories and stories for a lifetime. Experiences are created that combine with other life elements to shape our uniqueness. We don't mean that everyone should participate in daredevil stunts, but we all need to embrace the idea of risk in order to engage important life milestones. Think about the risks you take when travelling to foreign countries (considering language barriers), graduating, moving, and marrying. **Without risks, life is comfortable, but boring, unsuccessful, and unfulfilling.**

SCHEDULING FOR WORTHY RISKS

"Should I study right now, or should I give Ashley some advice? She is looking pretty sad...buuuut I said I would be finished with this task in one hour because I am suppose to move on to my next assignment by 7:00..."

> • • •
> *W*ITHOUT RISKS,
> LIFE IS COMFORTABLE,
> BUT BORING,
> UNSUCCESSFUL, AND
> UNFULFILLING
> • • •

"Should I go to the movies Saturday night to have at least one fun activity this weekend, or should I go the extra mile and study to make sure I ace my chemistry test on Tuesday?..."

Even in the realm of school with all the boundaries we should set for ourselves, we have to weigh what is worth the risk of losing valuable time. We also have to be wise about how we avoid suffering for these time losses. As we learn how to be disciplined people with great time management skills, **we need to know when it's worth it to allow delays in our schedules.** Routines that aid discipline and productivity are necessary, but at what point should we deviate from even the most efficient routine? One scheduling tip to always remember is the following: **The most efficient schedules have breathing room.** You can deviate from the plan and still yield the same results when you schedule properly. This involves planning ahead.

For example, although I could wait until tomorrow to complete this homework assignment that is not due until the day after tomorrow, I should do it today. I might be assigned

• • •

*T*HE MOST EFFICIENT SCHEDULES HAVE BREATHING ROOM

• • •

additional work from another class tomorrow, have an emergency, be called to an important meeting, or just be so exhausted that I cannot effectively complete the work with clarity of mind. If I see a girl crying on the bench on my way to do schoolwork, the worthy risk of helping her would not cause me to miss my assignment deadline *if* **my schedule is designed so that my work is completed**

far before the deadline instead of when the deadline arrives.

Another worthy risk for us was taking more time for ourselves on our weekends to achieve greater physical health, relaxation, and contentment during our college journey. Something clearly needed to change because we were so stressed and sick from all work and no play that we were not content. As simple as it sounds, we learned that we have to take time to unwind and enjoy life. For us, this was a risk because we were unsure of how we would maintain our grades if we changed our weekend habits. We thought, "Won't less time working mean more points deducted?"

Scheduling recreation time is worth the risk of spending less time (not no time, of course) on schoolwork during the weekend. Initially, we thought all the excess study during the weekend (except during church hours on Sundays) was necessary to keep 4.0's, but we discovered that the risk of surrendering some of that time was worth the additional joy, peace, and contentment in our educational journey. Even with our scheduled recreation, we were still able to go the extra mile in all of our classes and be over-prepared and confident. Following God's lead for this risk yielded retention of 4.0 GPA's + JOY!

OUR WORTHY RISK

"Don't people say that their GPA always gets lower when they study abroad? The teaching style is so different… You are in a brand new place, experiencing culture shock. You are spending most of your energy just trying to get used to living there. Because there is so much adventure outside in that new world, how can you focus on studies inside? I heard that Amanda went to Australia and had such a negative and lonely experience that she was depressed and homesick the whole time…so many factors to consider… Are you sure you want to go?"

Studying abroad in Milan, Italy—talk about a worthy risk! This experience during fall semester of our junior year was one of the best worthy risks in our lives so far. People told us that studying abroad could cause students' GPA's to decline, which was a scary thought for us. One day, we came to the conclusion that, even if our GPA altered slightly (as in one or two points ☺), studying abroad was a worthy risk. This three and a half month experience in a foreign country ended up being our best semester in college up to that point! It was beyond our comfort zone, yet amazing.

Before this time, whenever we had heard of students studying abroad, we thought such an endeavor was only for "those adventurous kind of people." The idea seemed unlike us, and very frightening. How could a student travel far away from home and live in a foreign culture away from friends, family, and a familiar school environment for an entire semester? We had probably done more international traveling than the average student our age, but the idea of living in a different country for that length of time was intimidating.

From the beginning of our college career until our junior year, Spelman repeatedly exposed us to the idea of studying abroad. The school presented panels of students to share their experiences, and held discussions to promote study abroad. Eventually, one of us began to feel drawn to the idea. The interest increased tremendously when the discussion was brought to our very own department, the music department.

By this time, only one of us (Kirstie) felt that studying abroad was a once in a lifetime adventure that we must experience before graduation. A sense of inward pressure insisted that regret would follow if we allowed the opportunity to pass by. This feeling urged Kirstie to hurry and obtain information to apply. While one was growing more and more excited about the idea, the other was becoming nervous at the thought of actually following through with it. After some persuading, Kristie agreed to pursue studying abroad.

During our time abroad, we gained academic and musical development. We studied music performance, Italian language, opera history, and classical voice. We gained an entirely new perspective of classical music while studying there! Because Europe is the home of classical music and Italy is the birthplace of opera, this music was all around us and was presented with the utmost vigor. The teachers were extremely passionate and opened our eyes to how we can interpret the music ourselves and express it uniquely. Our performance technique and confidence skyrocketed during this time. We became excited about opera like never before.

In the various places we traveled while abroad, we noticed the widespread appreciation for music, even classical (which many Americans underappreciate). We heard beautiful music from strangers while riding the metro, walking downtown, and even while walking down random alleys. When we told people in America that we were studying music in school, we often received responses like, "Oh, ok. That's nice." It seemed as if they were saying in their heads, "They're too smart to waste time and money studying music. How disappointing!" In Europe, the responses were more like, "WOW! You study music?! I wish I had the talent to do that!" With the increased music appreciation, top-notch teaching, and abundant exposure, our time abroad greatly expanded us as musicians.

While living in Milan, we also gained noticeable personal development. For the first time, we were separated! We stayed in two separate apartment buildings and had to ride the metro to get to one another. We learned a great deal about independence, a global mindset, and open-mindedness. We learned just how well we could function apart from one another after being together all of our lives. We also realized just how much we really do enjoy each other's company, proven by the way one of us would often take the metro just to go and cook with the other. Absence truly does make the heart grow fonder!

Although we lived in Milan, we traveled a great deal. We visited Venice, Rome, Aosta, Sicily, and Florence (Italian cities); Paris, France; Athens, Greece; Barcelona, Spain; and Dublin, Ireland. Interestingly enough, we had never booked a flight, train ride, or hotel before this semester. Our first time making these kinds of reservations was there in Italy in the Italian language! Right at our fingertips were the opportunities we had dreamed of…ones we'd assumed wouldn't happen until much later in life.

Although we had been privileged to travel many places (nationally and internationally) with our family, traveling independently without parental guides was very special. We were able to cross so many places off our "bucket list" that we had to scratch our heads and think about where else we would even want to go later in life. This study abroad experience stretched our thinking beyond what we could have imagined; provided us with stories and adventures to serve as fascinating conversation pieces; and developed us mentally, emotionally, spiritually, culturally, and musically. And again, following God's lead on which risk to take, we had this great experience, AND our 4.0's returned with us! ☺

SAYING YES!

Even during the precious weekdays that we teach should be reserved only for academics, relevant organization involvement, and a mid-week church service, there are exceptions. **Be flexible**

to stretch beyond your comfort zone and say yes to important opportunities and invitations. For example, we used to say "no" to everything that was happening during the school week. Then, we got opportunities such as speaking to a group of young ladies at Atlanta Metropolitan College. Although it sounds extremely unlike us to do this during our weekdays, we went on a Tuesday in the middle of the day (*after* class, of course). It was also in the middle of the day when we spoke to a group of young ladies at a high school. These experiences were not only rewarding for us, but also enriching to others. Remember the importance of taking advantage of great opportunities. Investment in important relationships, ministry, and helping people is worth the risk of deviation from the normal schedule sometimes.

UNWORTHY RISKS

Notice!—**Not every risk is worth taking!** Some financial investments are not worth the risk, as well as activities that involve sin in the name of being daring, edgy, or intentionally rebellious. Having pre-marital sex is not worth it, trying drugs isn't worth it, and testing your alcohol limit isn't worth it, among a number of other unworthy risks. Wildness does not have to be the opposite of bondage. Being so limitless that your grades suffer is not worth it. Making unwise decisions concerning time, morals, and relationships is always unworthy, even if it is fun at the moment. When you feel a tugging inside telling you not to take a particular risk (as long as it is not just fear), or if a wise person who loves you advises you not to take the risk, generally, DON'T.

If you really want to know what risks you should or should not take, run it by God! The Bible says that where the Spirit of the Lord is, there is liberty (II Cor. 3:17). Those who walk in this liberty in Christ follow His guidelines that He made for us out of His love and knowledge of all things past, present, and future. They choose to live by God's standards because they love Him, want to please Him, and trust Him. They trust that every guideline He sets is for our protection and greater good, just as a loving parent tells his/her child not to do "fun" stuff like playing in the street, running in the dark, or experimenting with the iron. **When you learn how to recognize the leading of God, you can more clearly know the difference between a worthy risk and an imminent disaster.**

CHALLENGE

1. Identify two risks you have taken that would be considered unworthy risks. What made them not worth it? What will you do in the future when faced with the same decisions?

2. Identify two risks that were worthy risks but that you were too afraid to take advantage of. What did you miss as a result of your decision?

3. Identify a risk that you can currently take advantage of and make a list of pros and cons. If the only con is fear, do it!

CHAPTER 11

$\mathscr{M}$IRACLES IN THE CLASSROOM:

Seeking the Source

KEY: PRAY HARD AND WORK HARD!

Miracles in the classroom?! Yes, they exist. We experienced them, and so can you! In one of our classes, we studied thoroughly and memorized everything the teacher told us that the first test would cover. Nevertheless, some of the first few questions on the test were over information she did not instruct us to study, nor was it printed in the book. It was merely information she said in her introduction on the first day of class, which none of the class deemed important. Kinda like that stuff when you're like, "Okay, okay, let's get to the content already, blah, blah, blah..." (in your head, of course...) Still, both of us had studied hard and prayed for one hundreds, even after we read some questions on the test (short answer, not multiple choice) and neither of us knew the answers.

Just so you know, this was a conversation we had after the class (not during the test) to find out that we both had the same experience. The answer to the question many of you may have is "NO," we did not cheat in order to make the same grades in college. Because we studied the same information for the same length of time, we happened to know the same answers and miss the same answers usually. So, back to the story…

Anyway, after praying again and resuming the test, God gave both of us the correct answers in the correct terminology! Understand, we had no clue what the correct answers were until we received our tests back with one hundreds! This was the very first quiz in this class, by the way. Also, we looked back at the notes from the first day (since we always take thorough notes, whether we think the information is important or not). Sure enough, the information was on our first page of notes. The answers that we had not studied, had not heard since the first day of class, and did not remember (but God gave to us during the quiz) were written on the quiz in the exact wording that the teacher had originally used on the first day of class. Of course, we were thinking, "Wow, verbally giving us the information only once, the first day of class, and expecting us to remember…? Huh?" Nonetheless, we were both astounded by the miracle that God had given us!

PRAYING FOR THE "LITTLE" THINGS?...

Similar to the instance above, we had many experiences in college that proved to be supernatural. As we diligently prayed, God would give us answers to the questions our thorough study could not have covered and our own minds could not have remembered. Some things people don't pray for because they don't think that it is possible.

For instance, many people don't think to pray for factors such as energy. Energy seems so simple and small, but its presence or lack thereof can have such a great impact on our productivity and well-being. With prayer, we have had more energy after three hours of sleep than we have had after eight hours of sleep without prayer. Simply pray and believe that God will bless the sleep you do receive and use it to bring restoration and rejuvenation to your body (Of course, use wisdom, and don't make a habit of sleep deprivation. This is for emergency use!).

There was a young lady who looked extremely drained in a meeting one night after glee club rehearsal. She looked as if her very soul were exhausted! When we talked to her afterwards, she expressed her overwhelming stress because of schoolwork, extracurricular obligations, and a build-up of mandatory community service hours needed to keep her scholarship. She had been surviving off of a few hours of sleep each night (for a while), and she did not know how she could continue without enough energy to accomplish everything that must be done.

When we asked her if she ever thought to ask God for energy, she responded with the expected, "No." After we gave her words of wisdom and encouragement, we challenged her to pray and truly believe that God would give her divine energy the next day. We told her that, upon waking up the next morning, she should hop out of the bed, jump up-and-down, and enthusiastically declare, "Thank you, Lord, for energy!" Although this might sound silly, which it sort of was at the time, it was an act of faith. She actually followed our advice and came running to us the next day with the most refreshing smile…a smile we had not seen on her face in a while! She exclaimed, "God did it! He answered my prayer! I had more energy throughout my day today than I have had in SO long!" **The power and importance of prayer are evident in the smallest and largest matters.**

PRAYING FOR EVERYTHING

Prayer changes things! Some think, "Well it's nice to pray and all… but what does that really do? It's probably more psychological relief than physical change and transformation…" Think of prayer like sowing seeds… If it is in God's perfect will, your prayer time is an investment for change!

We prayed before every quiz, test, paper, and project! We even prayed before studying and doing homework so that God would help us to focus on the right information. He answered! **When you work hard and pray hard, God's grace can cover the areas that you cannot predict on your own.**

Remember that there is nothing too trivial for you to pray about. Seriously, this might sound funny, but we sometimes pray about the weather! There have been times when we prayed that there would be clear blue skies, a nice warm breeze, no precipitation, and warm, but comfortable temperatures. For our outdoor birthday celebration, we might pray this prayer weeks in advance! Despite what the weather forecast looked like leading up to that day, our prayers were answered exactly! We felt so loved by God. He proved that He actually cared about those details of our lives...

• • •
*W*HEN YOU WORK HARD AND PRAY HARD, GOD'S GRACE CAN COVER THE AREAS THAT YOU CANNOT PREDICT ON YOUR OWN
• • •

Don't be fooled, though: not every prayer will be answered with a "yes". There are times when certain factors need to be the way they are. For example, the day that you might pray a "weather" prayer might be the day that God plans to use a storm to keep a plane from taking off that would have otherwise crashed that day. You wouldn't want hundreds of people to die while you are riding the Goliath roller coaster at Six Flags theme park, screaming "Weee!"

You never know… Have faith, but when you don't receive what you want, trust that He knows what's best.

God is not a genie, nor should He be treated as such. We are to build a relationship with Him and serve Him. The Bible says "… No good thing will He withhold from those <u>who walk uprightly</u>" (Psalm 84:11). It also says, "…how much more shall your Father which is in heaven give good things to them that ask him" (Matthew 7:11)? We serve Him because we love Him. He is our Father, and fathers, because of their love for their children, give to them. However, fathers say "no" sometimes. Unlike genies, fathers, including the Heavenly Father, love you enough to protect you with a "no" answer when necessary. The love that God has for us does not always give us what we want, but it gives us what we need.

CONNECTION YIELDING STRENGTH

The most important part of life is our connection to God. Let's imagine that you had a 4.0 GPA in school, got into the best graduate program, had a beautiful family, displayed impeccable fashion, and earned a six-figure income in a career you adored. This sounds like an amazing life here on this earth! Believe it or not, this is not enough. It would be somewhat sufficient (besides hopelessness during inevitable trials) if there were no afterlife to consider, but to have all of

• • •

THE ONLY CONSTANT IN THE EQUATION OF LIFE IS GOD

• • •

that and then spend eternity in Hell? What deceit! What a never-ending nightmare! You thought everything was perfect, but at the end of it all, the ultimate dread would be waiting for you.

Okay, let's back up for a second. So, before we get to the idea of the afterlife, do intelligence, family, and money breed happiness? If so, why do rich people with families commit suicide? Think about it. If money, family, good looks, and superior education can't make and keep you content in life, what can? Clearly, these things can't even give you peace that lasts. They can help, but they can't stand alone. What happens if you lose your job that brings you fulfillment and gives you a sense of purpose? What happens if a family member dies? Life is full of changes. **The only constant in the equation of life is God**. We have to be connected.

With this in mind, it would be silly for us to go about our days concentrating on all of the variables so much that we don't invest time in our relationship with God. Life doesn't get any richer than getting to know God intimately…His character, His ways, His desires, and His perfect plan for our lives. We don't even fully know what we were created for until we get to know the Creator. Who better to ask about the invention than the inventor? We discover these things in prayer, Bible study, and in time spent in God's presence. Without a relationship with Jesus Christ and without fulfilling His will, our lives cannot possibly be successful because we would be void of purpose.

In addition, we need God to help us in our daily lives to achieve all of our goals with optimal health and excellence. When you really walk with Him, He will guide you in everyday things that make a difference in your productivity.

Whether you are accustomed to focusing on your spirit or not, we are all spirit beings who need to take care of this significant part of our existence. We need daily spiritual rejuvenation that is available through daily devotion time with God. Prayer and Bible study can renew your thinking, relieve your stress, provide answers to your questions, and provide solutions to your problems.

You need these spiritual components to be able to transcend the frustrating and distracting details of life. Focusing on mundane things can make life seem overwhelming sometimes; but when you allow yourself to be consumed with God and everlasting things, even the biggest problems appear to shrink. With a refreshed mind everyday, which sleep alone cannot always provide, you are bound to focus better throughout the day and to be more productive.

OUR MISSION

When we picture holistic success, it should include true significance, which involves making a positive difference in the lives of others. When you know the keys to success, peace, joy, and love, it is only right to share it with others! Our world is polluted with so much hopelessness, pain, and wickedness that the need for salvation is evident. For those of us who are Christians, we are called to share the message of hope—Christ—with others because He brings healing, righteousness, peace, freedom, abundant life here on Earth, and eternal life beyond Earth. He is light even in the midst of darkness, and He is love personified. Fulfillment comes from Him and from fulfilling our charge to share Him with others (Mark 16:15).

As Christians, we should make ourselves available to God at school, work, and everywhere else. We can do this by talking to people about Christ, praying with people when they are receptive, praying *for* people more than we talk *about* them, and doing our best in all that we do. Remember that your life is your witness. Therefore, if you are sharing Christ, share His love in your lifestyle. Show yourself to be friendly (Proverbs 18:24), approachable, respectable, and kind.

Remember that you cannot use in the classroom, or anywhere else, something that you do not have. When you have a relationship with Christ, you can invoke miracles in the classroom and in life, on your behalf, and on the behalf of others. His Word teaches us how to live the right way, and that His blessings abound among those who do. Seeking the source of all wisdom, God, you can experience strength in your weakness, help in your distress, sufficiency in your lack, and even knowledge in your forgetfulness! Imagine opening your heart to Him completely, and having each of your voids filled in the absence of guilt or shame! Well, you can! Christ is the source of all that is excellent, so why not commit your life to Him?

CHALLENGE

1. For the next three days, play Christian worship music while you pray for at least 10 minutes and read at least one chapter in your Bible.

2. Write a list of things you don't normally pray about but you know you need God's help with. Begin praying for those things and including Him in your daily process.

3. If you have not received Christ as your Savior, or if you have stopped living for Him, we encourage you to pray the following prayer:

Lord, I believe in my heart, and I confess with my mouth that Jesus Christ is Lord. He died on the cross for my sins, and God raised Him from the dead. I now accept Christ as my personal Lord and Savior. I forgive everyone whom I have bitterness towards, and I ask that You forgive me for my sins. Thank You for Your grace and for saving me. Help me to grow daily in my relationship with You through diligent prayer and Bible study. Help me love what You love and hate what You hate, which is sin. Make me more like You, fill me with Your Holy Spirit, and help me love and serve You in a way that pleases You. In Jesus' name, amen.

CHAPTER 12

$\mathcal{N}$OW WHAT?...

Course Lessons to Life Lessons

KEY: LEARN THE LESSON; LIVE THE LESSON.

After being greeted by countless loving church people and relatives kissing our cheeks, squeezing our necks, and snapping our pictures at our graduation reception (at church, of course), it was time for vacation!

CELEBRATION

When we say that we like to work hard and play harder, we mean it! After graduation, we left early the next morning for a road trip to Florida with some of our best friends, and we had a blast! Between eating, sleeping, enjoying the beach, playing laser tag, and getting a taste of adventure at Wet N' Wild water park, we lived it up.

The unwinding process didn't stop there though... The very next week, we grabbed our passports and hopped on a plane to the Dominican Republic with our family! The most memorable experience in the Dominican was our caving excursion. Imagine being vertically lowered on a cable approximately 50 feet into the mouth of one of the largest caves in the world…walking and swimming through ice-cold water…travelling with only a tiny light on our hard hats while in the same quarters as snakes, tarantulas, and bats… This was an adventure full of memories that will last a lifetime!

Also while in the Dominican, we let our hair flow freely in the wind while horseback riding; we hiked in the beauty of nature; we went swimming in our private pool; and we enjoyed the climax of unwinding—eating and sleeping!

LIFE BEYOND

The week we returned, we got right back to the drawing board! We started working, and once again, we were extremely busy. Except, this time, for an even better cause! We continued striving for excellence in all that we do, while maintaining balance by investing in our relationships and making time for fun on the weekends.

WHEN YOU DO YOUR BEST IN SCHOOL AND BUILD YOUR BRIDGES VERSUS BURN THEM, OPPORTUNITIES WILL PRESENT THEMSELVES TO YOU!

We began to realize that these keys (of this book) to success in college (and life beyond) are for college AND life beyond. They are life principles. The principles that we applied in college are the same ones we use in our daily living. Therefore, we were not just preparing a trade or gaining academic knowledge in college, but we were preparing for life. Because of our extremely heavy workload in college, we had no choice but to learn how to multi-task and become experts at time management so that we could keep everything organized and remain on top of every class. We were juggling several classes (8, 9, 10 classes simultaneously and never fewer than 6), heavily involved in the glee club, regularly attending church, and serving as Sunday school teachers!

The connection between our college preparation (beyond academics) and our life after graduation is interestingly amazing! During college, we complained about having all of those evening engagements—glee club on Mondays, Wednesdays, and Fridays, and church on Thursdays. We even had Tuesday night commitments when we attended Christmas Carol and chamber singers rehearsals. Now, we conduct music rehearsals on Mondays and Wednesdays, host meetings and mentoring sessions on Tuesday evenings, sing and deliver the message for Thursday night services, and then lead Friday night youth socials! The practice of self-discipline, time management, and contentment in the journey was just the beginning of our life preparation.

Preparation for life *during* college eliminates the need to fear life *after* college. **When you do your best in school and build your**

bridges versus burn them, opportunities will present themselves to you! Because one of our friends (an international studies major) was diligent as a college student, she went to work overseas a few months after graduation. That amazing opportunity presented itself to her because she did her best while pursuing her degree. Another one of our good friends used to always say, "Oh girl, I'm not ready to graduate!" However, when she established her plan, which included the teaching program she would join after graduation, she became very excited about life after college.

For us, it was our diligence in school and God's grace that led to our title as double valedictorians. This title provoked all the media coverage, which led to numerous invitations for us to come and share our story!

Many people have asked if we are going to graduate school because of our perfect GPA's and exceptional study habits. To their surprise, we are not lovers of school!!! We simply value education, opportunities, and excellence. We will, however, go to graduate school if God leads us in that direction, as the seasons of our lives change, or as the need arises. If we go to graduate school, we are interested in earning a degree in counseling, psychology, or theology.

For now, we are extremely blessed, busy, and excited to be able to earn a living doing exactly what we are passionate about and gifted to do! Since graduation in 2013, we have been serving as the youth event coordinators at Word of Faith Family Worship Cathedral (WOF). In this position, we plan conferences, mentoring programs, spiritual retreats, customized programs, frequent weekend events, and more.

Although we had been actively leading in the music department at WOF since early teenage years, we officially became music directors (as written on our job description ☺) upon graduation. In that position, we lead worship, oversee the youth band, and teach the youth praise team and the 150-voice youth choir.

Additionally, we serve as the small group directors at WOF. In this position, we organize youth small group discipleship structures for the ministry, which we will eventually expand to include adult small groups.

In January 2014, we began serving as WOF's first 23-year-old female youth pastors! (Remember, we graduated from Spelman College in May 2013.) How exciting!

Thus far, by the grace of God, we have experienced much success in our youth ministry. Our Ignite Youth Ministry attendance has reached record numbers, drawing nearly 600 young people starting opening night! On the first night, over 60 students received salvation, and since then, God has continued to transform lives and create testimonies.

With the utmost honor and enthusiasm, we continue to receive and accept invitations as inspirational speakers/ministers at middle schools, high schools, alternative schools, mentoring programs, conferences, churches, non-profit organizations, and other events. We are also invited to sing at various programs, events, and services, and to bring our youth choir, youth praise team, and youth band to lead worship.

We love sharing our story, a.k.a. our testimony, to motivate others and equip them to achieve balance and success in every aspect of life through God, strategy, and hard work. We come alive when we are able to minister to others the very reason for our being and our success—Jesus Christ. We are loving life! Our lives are filled with meaningful relationships, God-given purpose, and joy, all because of our ever-present Help, Jesus Christ.

$\mathcal{A}$BOUT THE AUTHORS

Kirstie and Kristie Bronner are youth pastors, event coordinators, and music directors at Word of Faith Family Worship Cathedral in Austell, Georgia. They are passionate about mentoring young ladies, ministering through song and worship-leading, engaging students in academic settings using inspirational speaking, and ministering to youth, women, leaders, and church congregations. Kirstie and Kristie also specialize in teaching parents how to connect with their children, including specific teaching for pastors, their wives, and the PK's involved. They currently live together in Atlanta.

Ask questions, share testimonials, and invite Kirstie and Kristie to your events through their website kirstieandkristie.com, or email them at info@kirstieandkristie.com.

APPENDIX A

News Headline	Outlet Name	Outlet Type	News Date	Outlet State
100 WAPI - Birmingham's Talk FM - Georgia Twins to Graduate as Co-Valedictorians [From ABC News]	100wapi.com	Online, consumer	5/10/2013	
13WMAZ Eyewitness News at 11	13 WMAZ Eyewitness News at 11 PM - WMAZ-TV	Television program	5/11/2013	
14 News Sunrise at 4:30	14 News Sunrise - WFIE-TV	Television program	5/10/2013	
Twins named first college co-valedictorians	4029 TV		5/8/2013	
41 Action News Today	41 Action News Today - KSHBTV	Television program	5/10/2013	
8 News at 4:30 AM	8 News at 4:30 AM - WRIC-TV	Television program	5/10/2013	
8 News at Noon	8 News at Noon - WRIC-TV	Television program	5/10/2013	
ABC 7 News	ABC 7 News at 10 PM - WLSTV	Television program	5/9/2013	
Twins to Graduate With Identical Honors – Valedictorian	ABC News - Online	Online, news and business	5/10/2013	
Georgia Twins to Graduate as Co-Valedictorians	ABC News Radio - Online	Online, news and business	5/10/2013	
Georgia Twins to Graduate as Co-Valedictorians	AkronNewsNow.com	Online, consumer	5/10/2013	
Twins to Graduate as Co-Valedictorians	ArgentinaNews.net		5/10/2013	
Twin sisters named co-valedictorians at Spelman (Video)	Atlanta Business Chronicle - Online	Online, news and business	5/11/2013	
Twin Spelman Valedictorians Achieve Success with Balance	Atlanta Daily World		5/12/2013	
Twin Spelman Valedictorians Achieve Success with Balance	Atlanta Daily World - Online	Online, consumer	5/10/2013	
Twin Sisters Kirstie and Kristie Bronner Named Spelman Co-Valedictorians	Atlanta Daily World - Online	*Online, consumer*	5/7/2013	
Get Schooled with Maureen Downey	Atlanta Journal-Constitution - Online	*Online, news and business*	5/22/2013	

i

News Headline	Outlet Name	Outlet Type	News Date	Outlet State
Sister power: Twins are Spelman covaledictorians	Atlanta Journal-Constitution - Online	*Online, news and business*	5/21/2013	
Graduates Make Families, City Proud - Clark and Spelman Students Fulfill Academic Potential	Atlanta Voice - Online, The	Online, consumer	*5/24/2013*	G A
Twins to Graduate as Co-Valedictorians	BarcelonaNews.net		*5/10/2013*	
Twins to Graduate as Co-Valedictorians	BeijingNews.net		*5/10/2013*	
Bronner Twins Become Spelman's First Co- *Valedictorians*	*Black And Married With Kids*		*5/15/2013*	
Good News Friday: Spelman College Twins Become the School's First Co-Valedictorians	*Black Enterprise Magazine - Online*	Online, news and business	*5/10/2013*	NY
Meet Spelman College's Co-Valedictorians	*Black Entertainment Television (BET) - Online*	Online, consumer	*5/17/2013*	
Twins Graduate From Spelman as Co-Valedictorians in the Class of 2013	BlackNews.com		*5/13/2013*	
Identical Twins Named Co-Valedictorians For Spelman College	*Bossip*	Blog, consumer	5/9/2013	NY
Twins to Graduate as Co-Valedictorians	BritainNews.net		*5/10/2013*	
Twins to Graduate as Co-Valedictorians	BruineiNews.net		*5/10/2013*	
First Identical Twins Named Co-Valedictorians for Spelman College, Class of 2013	*Cascade Patch*	*Online, consumer*	5/8/2013	G A
Ch 2 Action News @ Noon	*Channel 2 Action News at Noon - WSB-TV*	*Television program*	*5/19/2013*	G A

News Headline	Outlet Name	Outlet Type	News Date	Outlet State
Twins named first college co-valedictorians Identical twins Kirstie and Kristie Bronner likely share many things in life. Now, the sisters also share the unique honor of being named covaledictorians for the Spelman College Class of 2013.	Click Orlando		5/8/2013	
Identical Twins Become Spelman College Co-Valedictorians	Clutch Magazine		5/9/2013	
WSAV News 3 Coastal Sunrise at 5:30	Coastal Sunrise at 5 AM - WSAV-TV	Television program	5/10/2013	GA
Newsradio 910 WSBA - The News Leader - Georgia Twins to Graduate as Co-Valedictorians [From ABC News]	Community Focus - WSBA-AM		5/11/2013	
NEWS: TWIN SISTERS BECOME SPELMAN'S FIRST CO-VALEDICTORIANS	Concrete Loop	Blog, consumer	5/13/2013	
Black Kos, Week In Review	DAILY KOS	Blog, news and business	5/17/2013	CA
Bronner Twins achieve identical success at Spelman College (part. 1)	Datzhott Where Everything Cool Is Hott		5/17/2013	
ABC World News With Diane Sawyer	Fairbanks CW	Television station	5/10/2013	AK
First News at 5:30	First News at 4:30 AM - KMBCTV	Television program	5/19/2013	MO
FOX 8 News @ 10	Fox 8 News at 10 PM - WVUETV	Television program	5/11/2013	LA
Fox Morning News	Fox Morning News at 7 AM - WFXB-TV	Television program	5/10/2013	SC
News Talk 770 AM / 92.5 FM WVNN - Georgia Twins to Graduate as Co-Valedictorians [From ABC News]	Fred and Peter in the Morning WVNN-AM		5/10/2013	
Georgia Gang	Georgia Gang - WAGA-TV	Television program	5/26/2013	GA
Good Day Alabama 5a	Good Day Alabama at 5 AM - WBRC-TV	Television program	5/10/2013	AL

News Headline	Outlet Name	Outlet Type	News Date	Outlet State
Good Day Lubbock	*Good Day Lubbock - KJTV-TV*	*Television program*	*5/10/2013*	TX
Good Morning Colorado	*Good Morning Colorado - KRDO-TV*	*Television program*	*5/10/2013*	CO
Good Morning Jacksonville Sunrise	*Good Morning Jacksonville Sunrise - WTLV-TV*	*Television program*	*5/10/2013*	FL
Good Morning Region 8 at 5AM	*Good Morning Region 8 at 5 AM - KAIT-TV*	*Television program*	*5/13/2013*	AR
8 News 5:30 AM	*Good Morning Richmond - WRIC-TV*	*Television program*	*5/10/2013*	VA
Good Morning San Diego Weekend	Good Morning San Diego at 7 AM - KUSI-TV	*Television program*	*5/11/2013*	CA
Georgia Twins to Graduate as Co-Valedictorians	GoWatertown.net	*Online, consumer*	*5/10/2013*	SD
Kirstie and Kristie Bronner Named Co- Valedictorians for Spelman College Class of 2013	Hawaii News Now	*Online, consumer*	*5/6/2013*	HI
BEAUTIFUL NEWS: Identical Twins Kristie & Kirstie Bronner Make Spelman History	Hello Beautiful	*Blog, consumer*	*5/9/2013*	NY
Twins to Graduate as Co-Valedictorians	JakartaNews.net		*5/10/2013*	
TalkRadio 790 KABC - Georgia Twins to Graduate as Co-Valedictorians [From ABC News]	KABC-AM - Online	*Online, consumer*	*5/10/2013*	CA
ABC World News With Diane Sawyer	KABC-TV	*Television station*	*5/10/2013*	CA
ABC World News With Diane Sawyer	KAEF-TV	*Television station*	*5/10/2013*	CA
ABC World News With Diane Sawyer	KAPP-TV	*Television station*	*5/10/2013*	WA
ABC World News With Diane Sawyer	KATU-TV	*Television station*	*5/10/2013*	OR
Twins to Graduate as Co-Valedictorians	KazakhstanNews.net		*5/10/2013*	

News Headline	Outlet Name	Outlet Type	News Date	Outlet State
KBOI News/Talk - Georgia Twins to Graduate as Co-Valedictorians [From ABC News]	KBOI-AM - Online	Online, consumer	5/10/2013	ID
Twins named first college co-valedictorians Identical twins Kirstie and Kristie Bronner likely share many things in life. Now, the sisters also share the unique honor of being named covaledictorians for the Spelman College Class of 2013.	KCCI-TV		5/9/2013	
Twins named first college co-valedictorians	KCRA-TV - Online	Online, consumer	5/8/2013	CA
The Mighty 920 KDHL-AM - Georgia Twins to Graduate as Co-Valedictorians [From ABC News]	KDHL-AM - Online	Online, consumer	5/11/2013	MN
ABC World News With Diane Sawyer	KDRV-TV	Television station	5/10/2013	OR
ABC World News With Diane Sawyer	KERO-TV	Television station	5/10/2013	CA
ABC World News With Diane Sawyer	KESQ-TV	Television station	5/10/2013	CA
Twins named first college co-valedictorians	KESQ-TV - Online	Online, consumer	5/8/2013	CA
ABC World News With Diane Sawyer	KEYT-TV	Television station	5/10/2013	CA
Twins named first college co-valedictorians	KEYT-TV - Online	Online, consumer	5/8/2013	CA
ABC World News With Diane Sawyer	KEZI-TV	Television station	5/10/2013	OR
ABC World News With Diane Sawyer	KFBB-TV	Television station	5/10/2013	MT
Kirstie and Kristie Bronner Named Co- Valedictorians for Spelman College Class of 2013	KFJX-TV - Online	Online, news and business	5/6/2013	KS
Kirstie and Kristie Bronner Named Co- Valedictorians for Spelman College Class of 2013	KFMB-AM (760 AM Talk Radio) - Online	Online, consumer	5/6/2013	CA
Kirstie and Kristie Bronner Named Co- Valedictorians for Spelman College Class of 2013	KFMB-FM (Jack FM) - Online	Online, consumer	5/6/2013	CA

News Headline	Outlet Name	Outlet Type	News Date	Outlet State
Georgia Twins to Graduate as Co-Valedictorians	*KFOR-AM - Online*	*Online, consumer*	*5/10/2013*	N E
ABC World News With Diane Sawyer	*KFSN-TV*	*Television station*	*5/10/2013*	CA
ABC World News With Diane Sawyer	*KGO-TV*	*Television station*	*5/10/2013*	CA
ABC World News With Diane Sawyer	*KGTV-TV*	*Television station*	*5/10/2013*	CA
ABC World News With Diane Sawyer	*KGUN-TV*	*Television station*	*5/10/2013*	AZ
Twins named first college co-valedictorians	*KHBS-TV - Online*	*Online, consumer*	*5/8/2013*	AR
Kirstie and Kristie Bronner Named Co- Valedictorians for Spelman College Class of 2013	*KHGI-TV - Online*	*Online, consumer*	*5/6/2013*	N E
ABC World News With Diane Sawyer	*KIFI-TV*	*Television station*	*5/10/2013*	I D
Twins named first college co-valedictorians	*KIFI-TV - Online*	*Online, consumer*	*5/8/2013*	I D
ABC World News With Diane Sawyer	*KIVI-TV*	*Television station*	*5/10/2013*	I D
ABC World News With Diane Sawyer	*KJCT-TV*	*Television station*	*5/10/2013*	CO
Twins named first college co-valedictorians	*KJCT-TV - Online*	*Online, consumer*	*5/9/2013*	CO
ABC World News With Diane Sawyer	*KJUD-TV*	*Television station*	*5/10/2013*	A K
Kirstie and Kristie Bronner Named Co- Valedictorians for Spelman College Class of 2013	KLJB-TV - Online	Online, consumer	*5/6/2013*	I A
Twins named first college co-valedictorians	*KMIZ-TV - Online*	*Online, consumer*	*5/8/2013*	M O
KMPH News Midday	*KMPH News Midday - KMPHTV*	*Television program*	*5/10/2013*	CA
Georgia Twins to Graduate as Co-Valedictorians	*KNEB-AM - Online*	*Online, consumer*	*5/10/2013*	N E
ABC World News With Diane Sawyer	*KNXV-TV*	*Television station*	*5/10/2013*	AZ
ABC World News With Diane Sawyer	*KOAT-TV*	*Television station*	*5/10/2013*	N M
Twins named first college co-valedictorians	*KOAT-TV - Online*	*Online, consumer*	*5/8/2013*	N M

News Headline	Outlet Name	Outlet Type	News Date	Outlet State
Twins named first college co-valedictorians	*KOCO-TV - Online*	*Online, consumer*	*5/8/2013*	OK
ABC World News With Diane Sawyer	*KOHD-TV*	*Television station*	*5/10/2013*	OR
ABC World News With Diane Sawyer	*KOMO-TV*	*Television station*	*5/10/2013*	WA
KOMU News Today	*KOMU 8 News Today - KOMUTV*	*Television program*	*5/10/2013*	MO
ABC World News With Diane Sawyer	*KOTA-TV*	*Television station*	*5/10/2013*	SD
Kirstie and Kristie Bronner Named Co- Valedictorians for Spelman College Class of 2013	*KOTV-TV - Online*	*Online, consumer*	*5/6/2013*	OK
Kirstie and Kristie Bronner Named Co- Valedictorians for Spelman College Class of 2013	*KPHO-TV - Online*	*Online, consumer*	*5/6/2013*	AZ
Twins named first college co-valedictorians	*KPRC-TV - Online*	*Online, consumer*	*5/8/2013*	TX
Kirstie and Kristie Bronner Named Co- Valedictorians for Spelman College Class of 2013	*KPTM-TV - Online*	*Online, consumer*	*5/6/2013*	NE
Kirstie and Kristie Bronner Named Co- Valedictorians for Spelman College Class of 2013	*KPTV-TV - Online*	*Online, consumer*	*5/6/2013*	OR
Twins named first college co-valedictorians	*KQCA-TV*		*5/8/2013*	
ABC World News With Diane Sawyer	*KRCR-TV*	*Television station*	*5/10/2013*	CA
Twins named first college co-valedictorians	*KRCR-TV - Online*	*Online, consumer*	*5/8/2013*	CA
Twins named first college co-valedictorians	*KRDO-FM - Online*	*Online, consumer*	*5/8/2013*	
ABC World News With Diane Sawyer	*KRDO-TV*	*Television station*	*5/10/2013*	CO
106.9 KROC-Today's Best Music! - Georgia Twins to Graduate as Co-Valedictorians [From ABC News]	*KROC-FM*		*5/10/2013*	
Georgia Twins to Graduate as Co-Valedictorians	*KRVN-AM - Online*	*Online, consumer*	*5/10/2013*	NE

News Headline	Outlet Name	Outlet Type	News Date	Outlet State
Twins named first college co-valedictorians | News - Home	*KSAT-TV - Online*	*Online, consumer*	*5/9/2013*	TX
Twins named first college co-valedictorians Identical twins Kirstie and Kristie Bronner likely share many things in life. Now, the sisters also share the unique honor of being named covaledictorians for the Spelman College Class of 2013.	*KSBW*		*5/9/2013*	
KSFO-AM - Georgia Twins to Graduate as Co-Valedictorians [From ABC News]	*KSFO-AM - Online*	*Online, consumer*	*5/10/2013*	CA
Kirstie and Kristie Bronner Named Co- Valedictorians for Spelman College Class of 2013	*KSLA-TV - Online*	*Online, consumer*	*5/6/2013*	LA
Kirstie and Kristie Bronner Named Co- Valedictorians for Spelman College Class of 2013 - KSTC-TV, Channel 45 Lifestyle-	*KSTC-TV - Online*	*Online, consumer*	*5/6/2013*	MN
ABC World News With Diane Sawyer	*KSVI-TV*	*Television station*	*5/10/2013*	MT
Kirstie and Kristie Bronner Named Co- Valedictorians for Spelman College Class of 2013	*KTEN-TV - Online*	*Online, consumer*	*5/6/2013*	TX
ABC World News With Diane Sawyer	*KTKA-TV*	*Television station*	*5/10/2013*	KS
ABC World News With Diane Sawyer	*KTMF-TV*	*Television station*	*5/10/2013*	MT
ABC World News With Diane Sawyer	*KTNV-TV*	*Television station*	*5/10/2013*	NV
Twins named first college co-valedictorians | Local News - Home	*KTVM-TV - Online*	*Online, consumer*	*5/8/2013*	MT
Twins named first college co-valedictorians	*KTVZ-TV - Online*	*Online, consumer*	*5/8/2013*	OR
ABC World News With Diane Sawyer	*KTWO-TV*	*Television station*	*5/10/2013*	WY
Twins named first college co-valedictorians | Nation/World News - Home	*KTXS-TV - Online*	*Online, consumer*	*5/8/2013*	TX

News Headline	Outlet Name	Outlet Type	News Date	Outlet State
Kirstie and Kristie Bronner Named Co- Valedictorians for Spelman College Class of 2013	KUAM-TV - Online	Online, consumer	5/6/2013	GU
Kirstie and Kristie Bronner Named Co- Valedictorians for Spelman College Class of 2013	KUSI-TV - Online	Online, consumer	5/6/2013	CA
ABC World News With Diane Sawyer	KVIA-TV	Television station	5/10/2013	TX
Twins named first college co-valedictorians	KVIA-TV - Online	Online, consumer	5/8/2013	TX
Kirstie and Kristie Bronner Named Co- Valedictorians for Spelman College Class of 2013	KWES-TV - Online	Online, news and business	5/6/2013	TX
Kirstie and Kristie Bronner Named Co- Valedictorians for Spelman College Class of 2013	KWTV-TV - Online	Online, news and business	5/6/2013	OK
ABC World News With Diane Sawyer	KWYB-TV	Television station	5/10/2013	MT
ABC World News With Diane Sawyer	KXLY-TV	Television station	5/10/2013	WA
Twins named first college co-valedictorians	KXLY-TV - Online	Online, consumer	5/8/2013	WA
ABC World News With Diane Sawyer	KXTV-TV	Television station	5/10/2013	CA
ABC World News With Diane Sawyer	KYUR-TV	Television station	5/10/2013	AK
KZEL-FM - Georgia Twins to Graduate as Co-Valedictorians [From ABC News]	KZEL-FM - Online	Online, consumer	5/11/2013	
Let's Talk Live	Let's Talk Live! - Newschannel 8	Cable/ satellite program	5/10/2013	VA
Georgia Twins to Graduate as Co-Valedictorians	Mason County Daily News		5/10/2013	
Spelman Twins Make History As School's First Co- Valedictorians	Michigan Chronicle - Online	Online, news and business	5/13/2013	MI
Morning Report	Morning Report - Newschannel 8	Cable/ satellite program	5/10/2013	VA

News Headline	Outlet Name	Outlet Type	News Date	Outlet State
WOKQ - New England's Best Country - Georgia Twins to Graduate as Co-Valedictorians [From ABC News]	Morning Waking Crew - WOKQ-FM	Radio program	5/10/2013	NH
Twin Sisters Kirstie and Kristie Bronner Named Spelman Co-Valedictorians	New Pittsburgh Courier - Online	Online, consumer	5/7/2013	PA
WMBB Midday News	News 13 Midday News - WMBB-TV	Television program	5/10/2013	FL
News 13 Early Edition 5am	News 13 This Morning - WLOSTV	Television program	5/10/2013	NC
News Channel 25 @ 6:30	News Channel 25 at 6 PM - KXXV-TV	Television program	5/9/2013	TX
Newschannel 12 Morning	Newschannel 12 Morning - WJTV-TV	Television program	5/11/2013	MS
Newschannel 13 @ Noon	Newschannel 13 at Noon - KRDO-TV	Television program	5/10/2013	CO
ABC World News With Diane Sawyer	Newschannel 8	Cable/satellite - network/station	5/10/2013	VA
Newswatch 16 at 4:30 PM	Newswatch 16 at 4 PM - WNEP-TV	Television program	5/10/2013	PA
Twin Bronner sisters named co-valedictorians at Spelman College	On Common Ground News - Online	Online, consumer	5/7/2013	GA
Twins named first college co-valedictorians	Pegasus News	Online, news and business	5/9/2013	TX
Twins to Graduate as Co-Valedictorians	PhilippinesNews.net		5/10/2013	
Kirstie and Kristie Bronner Named Co- Valedictorians for Spelman College Class of 2013	PRWeb - Online	Online, news and business	5/6/2013	
The Bronners: Twin Success at Spelman	Root, The Washington Post	Online, consumer	5/13/2013	DC
Twins to Graduate as Co-Valedictorians	RussiaNews.net		5/10/2013	
Twins to Graduate as Co-Valedictorians	South KoreaNews.net		5/10/2013	

News Headline	Outlet Name	Outlet Type	News Date	Outlet State
Twins to Graduate as Co-Valedictorians	Sri LankanNews.net		*5/10/2013*	
Identical Twins Kirstie & Kristie Bronner Are Co- Valedictorians Of Spelman	TheFrisky.com	Blog, consumer	*5/9/2013*	
Identical twins Kirstie and Kristie Bronner named *Spelman co-valedictorians*	TheGrio.com	*Blog, consumer*	*5/14/2013*	NY
Twins to Graduate as Co-Valedictorians	TurkmenistanNews.net		*5/10/2013*	
Identical Twins Kirstie & Kristie Bronner Are Co-Valedictorians Of Spelman	UptownMagazine.com	*Online, consumer*	*5/10/2013*	NY
WABI TV5 News at 5	WABI TV5 News at 5 PM - WABI-TV	*Television program*	*5/10/2013*	ME
Kirstie and Kristie Bronner Named Co- Valedictorians for Spelman College Class of 2013	WAFB-TV - Online	*Online, consumer*	*5/6/2013*	LA
Kirstie and Kristie Bronner Named Co- Valedictorians for Spelman College Class of 2013	WAND-TV - Online	*Online, consumer*	*5/6/2013*	IL
Bronner Twins Named Co-Valedictorians For Spelman 2013 Graduation	WAOK-AM - Online	*Online, consumer*	*5/18/2013*	GA
Twins named first college co-valedictorians	WAPT-TV - Online	*Online, consumer*	*5/8/2013*	MS
Twins named first college co-valedictorians	WBAL-TV Online	*Online, consumer*	*5/8/2013*	MD
WBAP News / Talk 820AM & 96.7 FM - Georgia Twins to Graduate as Co-Valedictorians [From ABC News]	WBAP-AM - Online	*Online, consumer*	*5/10/2013*	
Kirstie and Kristie Bronner Named Co- Valedictorians for Spelman College Class of 2013 - FOX21- Entertaining Delmarva One Click at a Time	WBOC- TV (DT2 - FOX) - Online	*Online, consumer*	*5/6/2013*	MD
Tune In News	WBRZ-TV	*Television station*	*5/10/2013*	LA
Twins named first college co-valedictorians	WCTI-TV - Online	*Online, consumer*	*5/8/2013*	NC

News Headline	Outlet Name	Outlet Type	News Date	Outlet State
Twins named first college co-valedictorians	*WCVB-TV - Online*	*Online, consumer*	*5/8/2013*	MA
Twins named first college co-valedictorians | News - Home	WCYB-TV		*5/8/2013*	
Kirstie and Kristie Bronner Named Co- Valedictorians for Spelman College Class of 2013	*WDAM-TV - Online*	*Online, consumer*	*5/6/2013*	MS
Twins named first college co-valedictorians	*WDIV-TV - Online*	*Online, consumer*	*5/8/2013*	MI
Kirstie and Kristie Bronner Named Co- Valedictorians for Spelman College Class of 2013	*WDRB-TV - Online*	*Online, consumer*	*5/6/2013*	KY
Kirstie and Kristie Bronner Named Co- Valedictorians for Spelman College Class of 2013	*WDSI-TV - Online*	*Online, consumer*	*5/6/2013*	TN
Twins named first college co-valedictorians	*WDSU-TV - Online*	*Online, consumer*	*5/8/2013*	LA
WEBE 108 Connecticut's Best Music Variety - Georgia Twins to Graduate as Co-Valedictorians [From ABC News]	WEBE-FM		*5/10/2013*	
Twins named first college co-valedictorians	*WFMZ-TV - Online*	*Online, consumer*	*5/8/2013*	PA
Kirstie and Kristie Bronner Named Co- Valedictorians for Spelman College Class of 2013	*WFSB-TV - Online*	*Online, consumer*	*5/6/2013*	CT
Kirstie and Kristie Bronner Named Co- Valedictorians for Spelman College Class of 2013	*WGCL-TV - Online*	*Online, consumer*	*5/6/2013*	GA
102.3 The Talk Monster WGOW-FM - Georgia Twins to Graduate as Co-Valedictorians [From ABC News]	WGOW-FM	*Radio station*	*5/10/2013*	TN
ABC World News With Diane Sawyer	WHOI-TV	*Television station*	*5/10/2013*	IL
Kirstie and Kristie Bronner Named Co- Valedictorians for Spelman College Class of 2013	*WICU/WSEE - TV - Online*	*Online, consumer*	*5/6/2013*	PA
WINK News This Morning	*WINK News This Morning at 5 AM - WINK-TV*	*Television program*	*5/10/2013*	FL

News Headline	Outlet Name	Outlet Type	News Date	Outlet State
Twins named first college co-valedictorians	WISC-TV - Online	*Online, consumer*	*5/8/2013*	WI
Twins named first college co-valedictorians	WISN-TV - *Online*	*Online, consumer*	*5/8/2013*	WI
WJBD - National News - Georgia Twins to Graduate as Co-Valedictorians	*WJBD-AM/FM - Online*	*Online, consumer*	*5/10/2013*	IL
WJBF News Channel 6 at 5	*WJBF News Channel 6 at 5 PM - WJBF-TV*	*Television program*	*5/9/2013*	GA
WJBF News Channel 6 at Noon	*WJBF News Channel 6 At Noon - WJBF-TV*	*Television program*	*5/9/2013*	GA
News/Talk 760 WJR - Georgia Twins to Graduate as Co-Valedictorians [From ABC News]	*WJR-AM - Online*	*Online, consumer*	*5/10/2013*	MI
Twins named first college co-valedictorians	*WJXT-TV*		*5/8/2013*	
Twins named first college co-valedictorians	*WJXT-TV - Online*	*Online, consumer*	*5/8/2013*	FL
Spelman Twins Make History As School's First Co-*Valedictorians*	*WJYD-FM - Online*	*Online, consumer*	*5/9/2013*	OH
Kirstie and Kristie Bronner Named Co- Valedictorians for Spelman College Class of 2013	*WLAX-TV - Online*	*Online, consumer*	*5/6/2013*	WI
Kirstie and Kristie Bronner Named Co- Valedictorians for Spelman College Class of 2013	*WLTZ-TV - Online*	*Online, consumer*	*5/6/2013*	GA
WMAL : Where Washington Comes to Talk - Georgia Twins to Graduate as Co-Valedictorians [From ABC News]	*WMAL-AM - Online*	*Online, consumer*	*5/11/2013*	DC
Eyewitness News at Eleven: May 11, 2013	*WMAZ-TV - Online*	*Online, consumer*	*5/12/2013*	GA
Kirstie and Kristie Bronner Named Co- Valedictorians for Spelman College Class of 2013	*WMBB-TV - Online*	*Online, consumer*	*5/6/2013*	FL
Kirstie and Kristie Bronner Named Co- Valedictorians for Spelman College Class of 2013	*WMC-TV - Online*	*Online, consumer*	*5/6/2013*	TN

News Headline	Outlet Name	Outlet Type	News Date	Outlet State
Kirstie and Kristie Bronner Named Co- Valedictorians for Spelman College Class of 2013	WMDT-TV - Online	Online, consumer	5/6/2013	MD
Twins named first college co-valedictorians Identical twins Kirstie and Kristie Bronner likely share many things in life. Now, the sisters also share the unique honor of being named covaledictorians for the Spelman College Class of 2013.	WMTW-TV		5/9/2013	
Twins named first college co-valedictorians	WMUR-TV - Online	Online, consumer	5/8/2013	NH
ABC World News With Diane Sawyer	WNCF-TV	*Television station*	*5/10/2013*	AL
Homeschool twins college co-valedictorians	*WND.com*	*Online, consumer*	*5/20/2013*	OR
Homeschool twins college co-valedictorians	*WND.com*	*Online, consumer*	*5/20/2013*	OR
Kirstie and Kristie Bronner Named Co- Valedictorians for Spelman College Class of 2013	*WNEM-TV - Online*	*Online, consumer*	*5/6/2013*	MI
Kirstie and Kristie Bronner Named Co- Valedictorians for Spelman College Class of 2013	*WOIO-TV - Online*	*Online, consumer*	*5/6/2013*	OH
Kirstie and Kristie Bronner Named Co- Valedictorians for Spelman College Class of 2013	*WOLF-TV - Online*	*Online, consumer*	*5/6/2013*	PA
Kirstie and Kristie Bronner Named Co- Valedictorians for Spelman College Class of 2013	*WOWK-TV - Online*	*Online, consumer*	*5/6/2013*	WV
WQAD News 8 at 6:30	*WQAD-TV*	*Television station*	*5/9/2013*	IL
Kirstie and Kristie Bronner Named Co- Valedictorians for Spelman College Class of 2013	*WRIC-TV - Online*	*Online, consumer*	*5/6/2013*	VA
Spelman twins make history as school's covaledictorians	*WSB-TV - Online*	*Online, consumer*	*5/8/2013*	GA
Kirstie and Kristie Bronner Named Co- Valedictorians for Spelman College Class of 2013	*WSET-TV - Online*	*Online, consumer*	*5/6/2013*	VA

News Headline	Outlet Name	Outlet Type	News Date	Outlet State
Kirstie and Kristie Bronner Named Co- Valedictorians for Spelman College Class of 2013	WSHM-TV - Online	Online, consumer	5/6/2013	MA
Identical Twin Sisters Named Co-Valedictorians	WSOC-TV - Online	Online, consumer	5/15/2013	NC
Good Day Columbus at 6AM	WSYX-TV	Television station	5/10/2013	OH
Sports Xtra 1330 WTRX - Georgia Twins to Graduate as Co-Valedictorians [From ABC News]	WTRX-AM		5/11/2013	
Kirstie and Kristie Bronner Named Co- Valedictorians for Spelman College Class of 2013	WTVG-TV - Online	Online, consumer	5/6/2013	OH
WTVM Newsleader 9 @ Noon	WTVM Newsleader 9 at Noon - WTVM-TV	Television program	5/10/2013	GA
Kirstie and Kristie Bronner Named Co- Valedictorians for Spelman College Class of 2013	WUPV-TV - Online	Online, consumer	5/6/2013	VA
Kirstie and Kristie Bronner Named Co- Valedictorians for Spelman College Class of 2013	WWTV-TV - Online	Online, consumer	5/6/2013	MI
Twins named first college co-valedictorians Identical twins Kirstie and Kristie Bronner likely share many things in life. Now, the sisters also share the unique honor of being named covaledictorians for the Spelman College Class of 2013.	www.kmbc.com	.	5/9/2013	
Twins named first college co-valedictorians	www.wapt.com		5/8/2013	
Twins named first college co-valedictorians Identical twins Kirstie and Kristie Bronner likely share many things in life. Now, the sisters also share the unique honor of being named covaledictorians for the Spelman College Class of 2013.	www.wisn.com		5/9/2013	

News Headline	Outlet Name	Outlet Type	News Date	Outlet State
Twins named first college co-valedictorians Identical twins Kirstie and Kristie Bronner likely share many things in life. Now, the sisters also share the unique honor of being named covaledictorians for the Spelman College Class of 2013.	www.wpbf.com		5/9/2013	
Twins named first college co-valedictorians Identical twins Kirstie and Kristie Bronner likely share many things in life. Now, the sisters also share the unique honor of being named covaledictorians for the Spelman College Class of 2013.	www.wptz.com		5/9/2013	
Twins named first college co-valedictorians Identical twins Kirstie and Kristie Bronner likely share many things in life. Now, the sisters also share the unique honor of being named covaledictorians for the Spelman College Class of 2013.	www.wyff4.com		5/8/2013	
Spelman College names identical twins as co - valedictorians	WXIA-TV - Online	Online, consumer	5/10/2013	GA
Twins named first college co-valedictorians	WXII-TV		5/8/2013	
Twins named first college co-valedictorians	WXII-TV - Online	Online, consumer	5/8/2013	NC
Twins named first college co-valedictorians	WYFF-TV - Online	Online, consumer	5/8/2013	SC
Twin Spelman Valedictorians Graduate in Excellence!	Yahoo! Voices	Online, consumer	5/28/2013	NY